Letts

Framework
FOCUS

101

Red Hot

Maths
Starters

Kathryn

D1350379

Contents

Acknowledgements

I have been fortunate in meeting so many enthusiastic and inspiring maths teachers over the years and I owe my thanks to all of them. In particular, I would like to thank John Parsons of Winston Churchill School, Woking, for his input, creativity and inspiration. My thanks also go to Leanne Charles for her support and enthusiasm and my current maths colleagues at Eggbuckland Community College, Plymouth, who have encouraged me along the way.

Introduction

Introducing starters

As endorsed by the Key Stage 3 *Framework for Teaching Mathematics*, lessons are now taught in three parts. They should begin with a 10–15 minute starter, followed by the main part of the lesson and finally a plenary. The starter can occur in many forms, from a written activity to an oral one, with students working in groups, pairs or individually. This will largely depend on the size of your class and what you feel most comfortable with.

Target audience

This book is suitable for any maths teacher who wants to be inspired, including supply teachers, cover teachers and NQTs (even primary teachers may find the book a good source of ideas which they can adapt accordingly). In fact, this book is for any teacher who wants to bring an enjoyable, positive atmosphere for learning into the classroom, with minimum time spent planning it.

In reality – the timing of starters and when to use them

The starters in this book are supposed to be flexible. They can take as little as 10 minutes if you feel this is enough to get your point across or can be used in a longer session if you feel the students will benefit from more practice.

You may find that it's best to start the lesson with a topic that is different from the main part of the lesson to allow students to 'warm up'. On the other hand, it can be beneficial to start the lesson with an activity that is related to previous lessons, as it acts as a reminder and revision tool. Students often forget what they did a week ago and it's a great way of refreshing their memories.

Alternatively, these activities can be used when you feel the students are getting restless and in need of a change. Sometimes cover teachers arrive to lessons in need of something to get the class settled and focused before the cover work arrives.

You may even find that some of the starters could be used as a plenary activity to test the students' understanding at the end of the lesson. This is a particularly good idea for the noisier activities, as students leave your classroom excited rather than disrupting the main part of the lesson when you want them to do exercises in their books.

How to use this book

Contents grid

For simplicity, each starter has been assigned to one specific year group and one objective only. However, all the activities are extremely flexible. Most of them can be used for any Key Stage 3 year group and adapted according to your students' abilities. In reality, the activities also often cover more than one objective.

Objectives and aims

Each starter activity has been matched to an appropriate Key Stage 3 Framework objective and subsequent aim. However, I do feel that the main aim is for students to enjoy coming to maths lessons. I hope you will find it as rewarding as I do when they actually ask to play what is essentially a times table activity.

Resources

The activities require minimal resources. However, some activities are so much more fun with individual whiteboards, for example, and once bought, you can obviously use them over and over again. Undoubtedly, my personal favourite is the giant coloured foam die which can be used for most of the dice activities – football enthusiasts suddenly see maths in a new light!

Activities

The instructions for each activity are presented as short, bulleted action points, to minimise the time required for planning. Activities have been chosen that require no photocopying of additional material (except a few activities, which may benefit from a quick OHT being prepared beforehand).

Answers

Answers are provided on the same page as the questions to save valuable time spent leafing through the back pages. Several of the activities have numerous alternative answers, which leads to healthy discussion.

Differentiation

The up arrow (⇑) represents more challenging activities, whereas the down arrow (⇓) represents an easier version. However, some of the suggestions are really alternative versions of the activity, rather than being significantly harder or easier. Many of these ideas can be further adapted and can be used as a basis to inspire even more creative lessons.

Many teachers have a selection of great starter activities that they know work in the classroom. However, what many of us are lacking is a quick, portable reference book that we can use to refresh our memories and inspire ourselves from time to time. I started writing this book for the maths department at Winston Churchill School, Woking, because I found it frustrating that so many of our good ideas were, with time, forgotten.

I hope you enjoy using these 101 starters as much as my students and I do. Take care though, not to let on that students are actually 'learning without realising it'.

Enjoy!

Kathryn Stahl

Maths Rocks!

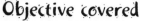

YEAR 7

Objective covered
Applying mathematics and solving problems
Solve word problems.

Aim
To encourage students to solve a word
problem mentally using visualisation.

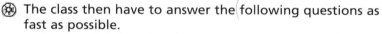

Activity

⚙ Ask the class to imagine the word MATHS with the word
ROCKS written directly below it:

M A T H S
R O C K S

⚙ The class then have to answer the following questions as
fast as possible.

1 What letter is above the C?

2 What letter is below the H?

3 What letter is diagonally to the right of the O?

4 What letter is diagonally to the left of the A?

5 If you substitute the H with another T and the R with
another S, what do the words read now?

Answers
1 T   2 K   3 T   4 R   5 MATTS SOCKS

Differentiation

⚙ ⬆ Present more than two words to the class for an extra challenge.
For example, add OKAY! underneath ROCKS so it reads:

M A T H S
R O C K S
O K A Y !

⚙ ⬇ Ask students to work in pairs to make up a similar word puzzle
for the class.

Memory game

Objective covered
Applying mathematics and solving problems
Solve word problems.

Aim
To encourage students to solve a word problem mentally using visualisation.

Activity

✸ Write the numbers 1 to 9 on the board in three rows:

1	2	3
4	5	6
7	8	9

✸ Ask students to study the numbers carefully for 1 minute and to think of questions that might be asked.

✸ When a minute is up, rub the numbers out and fire questions at the class:

1 What's the total of the middle column?

2 What's the sum of the top row?

3 What's the product of the middle row?

4 Swap the 9 with the 1. What's the sum of the bottom row now?

Answers
1 15   2 6   3 120   4 16

Differentiation

✸ ⬆ Use the numbers 1 to 16 in four rows.

✸ ⬆ Introduce algebra by replacing the middle number with *x* and asking students to give expressions for various rows and columns.

Make 13

Objective covered

Applying mathematics and solving problems
Solve word problems.

Aim

To practise identifying necessary information to solve a problem.

Activity

⊛ On the board, draw the following arrangement of boxes:

⊛ Ask students to then place each of the numbers 1 to 9 (once only) in the cells so that each of the four lines of three cells add up to 13.

Answer

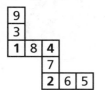

Differentiation

⊛ ⬆ Get students to discuss a good strategy for working this problem out (rather than relying on trial and improvement). They should realise that the sum of the totals for each of the four lines is 13 + 13 + 13 + 13 = 52. The sum of all the numbers in the grid is 45. The difference between these values, 52 – 45 = 7, must be the sum of the numbers used in more than one line. The only three numbers that add up to 7 are 1, 2 and 4, so these need to be positioned first.

⊛ ⬆ See if students can come up with an alternative solution.

Street madness

Objective covered
Applying mathematics and solving problems
Solve word problems.

Aim
To encourage students to solve a word problem by breaking a complex calculation into simpler steps.

Activity
⊛ Read out the following problem:

> The houses in a street are numbered from 1 to 100. How many figure 5s are there altogether in the house numbers?

⊛ Ask students to raise their hands when they think they've got the answer.

Answer
20

Differentiation
⊛ ⇑ Change to houses numbered from 1 to 1000. (Answer: 200)

⊛ ⇑ Change to houses numbered from 1 to 10 000. (Answer: 2000)

⊛ ⇑ Get students to find ways of adding the house numbers 1 to 100 by using an appropriate strategy (by pairing up 100s).

Skittles

Objective covered
Applying mathematics and solving problems
Solve word problems.

Aim
To encourage students to solve a word problem mentally using visualisation and improve their understanding of statistics.

Activity

- Ask the class to imagine that there are 9 skittles in a line in the following order: 4 red, 3 green, 2 yellow.

- The class then has to answer the following questions as fast as possible:

  1. What colour is the middle skittle?

  2. What colour is the 7th skittle from the left?

  3. Move 3 skittles from the left and put them on the right. What colour is the middle skittle now?

Answers
1 Green   2 Green   3 Yellow

Differentiation

- ⬆ Use more than 9 skittles and more colours.

- ⬆ Introduce terms such as qualitative data versus quantitative data.

- ⬆ Discuss how to find the position of the middle 'number' (median), i.e. $(n + 1) \div 2$. So for 9 items, the middle item would be in the $(9 + 1) \div 2 = 5$th place.

- ⬆ Discuss quartiles.

Unwise landlady?

Objective covered

Applying mathematics and solving problems
Explain and justify methods and conclusions.

Aim

To explore real-life connections in mathematics and practise the ability to compare and evaluate the results.

Activity

⊛ Discuss this statement made by one landlady to her tenant:

> 'I don't mind if you pay £50 rent per week
> or £200 per month, just so long as I get it!'

⊛ Ask students if there is a difference. Discuss with evidence.

Answers

£50 per week × 52 weeks in the year = £2600 p.a.
£200 × 12 months = £2400 p.a.
Paying monthly, the tenant would save £200 p.a.

Differentiation

⊛ ⬆ Ask students how much the tenant would save each year by paying £240 monthly as opposed to £60 per week. (£240 p.a.)

⊛ ⬆ Ask students to predict how much the tenant would save by paying £280 per month as opposed to £70 per week. (£280 p.a.)

Pyramidal products

Objective covered
Applying mathematics and solving problems
Solve more demanding problems.

Aim
To practise solving number problems by developing
an appropriate strategy.

Activity
❀ Using each of the numbers 1, 2, 4, 6, 8 and 12 once only,
see if students can fill in the boxes so that the product
of the three numbers on each side is 48.

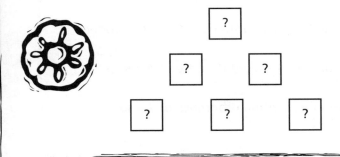

```
        ?
      ?   ?
    ?   ?   ?
```

Answer

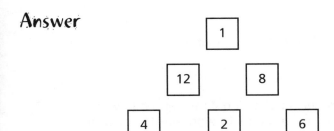

```
        1
     12    8
    4    2    6
```

Differentiation
❀ ⬆ Encourage students to notice that each of 1, 4 and 6 can be used
in two ways to make 48, whereas 2, 8 and 12 can each be used
only one way. This means 1, 4 and 6 must go in the corners.

Just two numbers

Objective covered

Applying mathematics and solving problems
Solve more demanding problems.

Aim

To practise solving number problems (including the use of negative numbers) and become familiar with associated vocabulary.

Activity

✷ Ask students to solve each of these number problems.

1 Find two numbers with a sum of 0.8 and a product of 0.15.

2 Find two numbers with a sum of –11 and a product of 28.

3 Find two numbers with a difference of 4 and a quotient of 3.

4 Find two numbers with a difference of 2 and a quotient of –1.

Answers

1 0.5 and 0.3   2 –7 and –4   3 6 and 2   4 –1 and 1

Differentiation

✷ ⇑ Let the two numbers in question 4 be a and b (giving $b - a = 2$ and $b \div a = -1$) and get students to work out the answer algebraically.

Two-faced cards

Objective covered
Applying mathematics and solving problems
Solve more demanding problems.

Aim

To practise solving number problems by developing an efficient strategy.

Activity

✸ Pose this problem to the class:

- The numbers 3 and 10 are written on the front of two cards.

- There is a different number on the back of each card.

- When the two cards are placed on a table, the sum of the two numbers showing can be any of the following: 12, 13, 14 or 15.

- What are the two numbers on the back of the cards?

Answer

2 is on the back of the number 3 card.
12 is on the back of the number 10 card.

Differentiation

✸ ⬆ Get students to think up their own question for the class to master.

Millennium bug

Objective covered

Applying mathematics and solving problems
Solve more complex problems by breaking them into smaller steps or tasks, choosing and using efficient techniques for calculation, and resources.

Aim

To encourage students to solve a word problem by breaking a complex calculation into simpler steps as well as practising calculations efficiently using a calculator.

Activity

⚙ Pose the following problem to the class:

'How can you make 1000 with eight 8s?'

Answer

$888 + 88 + 8 + 8 + 8$ or $(8 \times 8 + 8 \times 8) \times 8 - (8 + 8 + 8)$

Differentiation

⚙ ⬆ Discuss how you would use your calculator to get the second answer.

⚙ ⬆ Ask students whether they can reach 1000, in a similar way, using 7s.

⚙ ⬆ Discuss BODMAS.

⚙ ⬇ Get students to come up to the board and write a variety of ways of making 1000.

Crazy consecutives

Objective covered/aim

Applying mathematics and solving problems
Solve substantial problems by breaking them into simpler tasks.

Activity

⊛ See how quickly students can solve these problems and discuss how they did it.

   1   Which three consecutive integers add up to 96?

   2   Which three consecutive integers add up to 78?

   3   Which three consecutive integers add up to 87?

   4   Which four consecutive integers add up to 50?

   5   Which four consecutive integers add up to 126?

Answers

1   31, 32, 33   2   25, 26, 27   3   28, 29, 30
4   11, 12, 13, 14 5   30, 31, 32, 33

Differentiation

⊛ ⇑ If the sum of three consecutive integers is x, how do you find the three integers (in terms of x)?

(Answers: $\frac{x}{3} - 1, \frac{x}{3}, \frac{x}{3} + 1$ or $\frac{x-3}{3}, \frac{x}{3}, \frac{x+3}{3}$)

⊛ ⇑ If the sum of four consecutive integers is x, how do you find the four integers (in terms of x)?

(Answers: $\frac{x-6}{4}, \frac{x-6}{4} + 1, \frac{x-6}{4} + 2, \frac{x-6}{4} + 3$ or $\frac{x}{4} - 1\frac{1}{2}, \frac{x}{4} - \frac{1}{2}, \frac{x}{4} + \frac{1}{2}, \frac{x}{4} + 1\frac{1}{2}$)

⊛ ⇑ Ask students to think up their own question for three consecutive integers.

⊛ ⇑ Get them to think up their own question for four consecutive integers.

Make a century

Objective covered
Applying mathematics and solving problems
Solve substantial problems by breaking them into simpler tasks, using a range of techniques.

Aim
To encourage students to solve a problem, using trial and improvement or otherwise.

Activity
⊛ Ask students to put in some missing operation signs to make the following sum work:

1 2 3 4 5 6 7 8 9 = 100

Answer
$123 - 45 - 67 + 89$ or $123 - 4 - 5 - 6 - 7 + 8 - 9$

Differentiation
⊛ ⇓ Tell students they need to put in only three signs: one plus and two minuses.

⊛ ⇑ Ask students to come up with their own question for the class.

⊛ ⇑ Get them to devise a strategy for adding all the whole numbers from 1 to 100. (Hint: Try pairing $1 + 99$, $2 + 98$, etc. The answer is $100 \times 50 + 50 = 5050$). You could suggest they start by adding the numbers from 1 to 10 instead.

⊛ ⇑ Get students to type $20 + 40 \times 2$ into their calculators and see if they all get 100 (as opposed to 120). Discuss BODMAS.

Sounds impressive

Objectives covered
Applying mathematics and solving problems
Explore connections in mathematics.
Present a concise, reasoned argument.

Aim
To explore number connections in mathematics and appreciate the limitations and constraints of number patterns.

Activity
⊛ See if students can spot the trick for this group of sums:

   $23 \times 27 = 621$

   $43 \times 47 = 2021$

   $83 \times 87 = 7221$

   $55 \times 55 = 3025$

   $52 \times 58 = 3016$

   $54 \times 56 = 3024$

⊛ Ask students if they think the trick will work with all numbers.

Answers
For each calculation, multiply the common first digit by its next consecutive number. This gives the first answer digits. Then multiply the units digits together to get the remaining answer digits. So, for example, the first digit of 23×27 is $2 \times 3 = 6$ and the remaining digits are $3 \times 7 = 21$ giving $23 \times 27 = 621$.

This only works if the numbers to be multiplied have the same number of tens and their units add up to 10. Still, it sounds impressive if you can say at speed that $45^2 = 2025$!

Differentiation
⊛ ⇑ Using algebra, or otherwise, can students prove why it works?

Hidden differences

Objective covered

Place value, ordering and rounding
Understand and use place value.

Aim

To understand and use place value and practise rounding whole numbers to the nearest 10, 100 and 1000.

Resources

Number fans (not essential). To order a pack of thirty-five 0–9 petal-shaped number fans, phone 01392 384697 and quote Devon County Council purchasing catalogue number 45.5591.

Activity

❀ Put the following arrangement of numbers on the board:

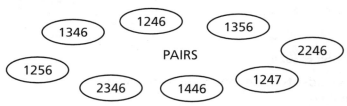

```
            1246          1356
   1346
                               2246
            PAIRS
  1256
       2346      1446    1247
```

❀ Get students to identify, as fast as possible (using number fans), how many pairs of numbers have a difference of:

   a 10   *b* 100   *c* 1000

Answers

a 2 pairs   *b* 4 pairs   *c* 2 pairs

Differentiation

❀ ⬇ In groups of three, get students to round each number to the nearest 10, 100 and 1000 using their number fans. (They will need to work together as a team as all three number fans will be needed when rounding to the nearest thousand.)

Think big

Objective covered

Place value, ordering and rounding
Understand and use place value.

Aim

To understand and use place value, in particular,
appreciating the position of a zero.

Resources

Playing cards numbered 1–9 and a joker representing zero.

Activity

⊛ The aim of the game is to create the largest number
   possible using a bit of knowledge on place value,
   probability and pure luck!

⊛ Show students the ten cards and pick one student to
   shuffle them.

⊛ Then get students to draw six boxes in a line:

   ▢ ▢ ▢ ▢ ▢ ▢

⊛ Draw cards from the pack, one at a time, without
   replacement. As each card is drawn, the students should fill
   in a box with the number showing.

⊛ The student(s) who fulfils the aim specified wins 1 point.

⊛ Play as many rounds as time allows.

Differentiation

⊛ ⇓ Less than 6 boxes could be used.

⊛ ⇑ More than 6 boxes could be used. Ask students to read their
   numbers.

⊛ ⇑ A decimal point could be inserted, say, in between the second
   and third box.

Fill in the blanks

Objective covered
Place value, ordering and rounding
Understand and use place value.

Aim
To understand and use place value as well as practise adding and subtracting positive integers.

Activity

⊛ On the board, draw 6 boxes as shown:

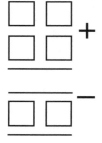

⊛ Students must use each of the numbers 1, 2, 4, 5, 7 and 9 once only to fill in the boxes. The aim is to get the largest possible answer to the sum (addition then subtraction).

⊛ Change the numbers and give students another go. You could get the class to choose them!

Answer
157 (94 + 75 – 12 or 74 + 95 – 12)

Differentiation
⊛ ⇑ Change the aim to 'find the smallest number'.
(14 + 25 – 97 = –58)

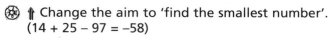

Two zeros to win

Objective covered
Place value, ordering and rounding
Understand and use place value.

Aim
To understand and use place value and standard column procedures to subtract positive integers as well as to practise rounding whole numbers to the nearest 10 and 100.

Resources
One ordinary die.

Activity
- Each student must choose two different three-digit numbers, without using zeros, for example, 236 and 135.
- Now roll the die.
- If the number thrown is 4, for example, students subtract 4, 40 or 400 from either of their original three-digit numbers. If the next number thrown is a 6, for instance, the student may take away 6, 60 or 600 from either of the 2 remaining numbers etc.
- The game is over when a student has reduced both of their numbers to exactly zero. (A great way to sneakily practise subtraction!)
- Students may miss a go only if the number thrown would give them a negative number.

Differentiation
- ⬆ Use a differently numbered die.
- ⬆ Get students, in turn, to choose the next number.

Nearly

Objectives covered/aims

Place value, ordering and rounding
Round positive numbers to any given power of 10.
Understand and use place value and practise reading large positive integers.

Resources

One ordinary die.

Activity

⊛ Decide on an aim, such as you win if you get the:

- lowest even number
- highest odd number
- highest multiple of 5
- nearest to 123 456
- nearest number to a millennium number.

⊛ Then get students to draw six boxes in a line:

☐ ☐ ☐ ☐ ☐ ☐

⊛ Roll the die six times. After each roll students should fill in a box with the number showing.

⊛ The student(s) who fulfils the aim specified wins 1 point.

⊛ Play as many rounds as time allows.

Differentiation

⊛ ⬆ Use a differently numbered die, such as 0–9.

Invisible number line

Objective covered

Integers, powers and roots
Understand negative numbers as positions on a number line.

Aim

To understand negative numbers as positions on a number line and practise visualisation.

Resources

A metre ruler or window pole.

Activity

- ✤ Bang the board in the centre at '0'. Continue to bang along the board to the right in equal steps. Students should shout out '1', '2', '3', ...

- ✤ At some point, change direction by banging back along the board to the left. Students should then count back along the 'invisible number line'. Continue back past '0' to include negative numbers.

- ✤ It becomes fun when you speed up a bit. Keep changing the direction of the count to catch as many students out as possible!

Differentiation

- ✤ ⬆ Count on and back in steps of 0.5. From time to time stop and ask students to call out the number needed to make the last number reach 1. For example, you call –2.5, they call 3.5.

It's hotting up

Objective covered

Integers, powers and roots
Understand negative numbers as positions on a number line.

Aim

To understand and visualise negative numbers as positions on a number line and practise adding and subtracting them in context.

Activity

⊛ Ask students to visualise a vertical thermometer.

⊛ Tell them that the temperature reads –2°C.

⊛ Ask the following questions.

1 What will the temperature be when it:

   a rises by 3°C

   b falls by 7°C

   c increases by 12°C

   d decreases by 2°C?

2 If the temperature this morning was –7°C and this afternoon it is 12°C, by how much has it risen?

Answers

1 a 1°C   b –9°C   c 10°C   d –4°C
2 19°C

Differentiation

⊛ ⬆ Get students to come up with a variety of sums if you tell them the final temperature is, say, –3°C.

Personalised number line

Objective covered

Integers, powers and roots
Understand negative numbers as positions on a number line.

Aim

To understand how negative numbers can be positioned on number lines of different scales/magnitudes.

Activity

⊛ Ask each student to write a number on a piece of paper (specify the range according to ability, such as whole numbers from −100 to −10).

⊛ Collect the pieces of paper and shuffle them. Choose, say, six of them.

⊛ Students then have to fit the six numbers on a blank number line, of your choice, on the board.

Differentiation

⊛ ⬆ Specify that students need to use decimals with one decimal place.

⊛ ⬇ Get the class to work in groups and give each group a set of six numbers to position on a number line.

Number search

Objective covered

Integers, powers and roots
Add positive integers.

Aim

To practise adding positive integers in context.

Resources

One ordinary die. Most effective with a giant coloured sponge die. To order, phone 01392 384697 and quote Devon County Council purchasing catalogue number H 71.4950, for a foam cube with dimensions of 155 mm.

Activity

- ⊛ Ask students to draw a 3 by 3 grid, so that they have 9 cells.

- ⊛ Roll the die 9 times. After each roll students should fill any one of their cells.

- ⊛ They then need to find as many connecting cells as they can that total 15 (connecting meaning next door, either horizontally or vertically but not diagonally).

- ⊛ Give a time limit of, say, 2 minutes.

Differentiation

- ⊛ ⬆ Change the grid size and/or rules, for example, diagonals only, find connecting cells that total 20, etc.

Negative loop game

Objective covered/aim
Integers, powers and roots
Add and subtract positive and negative integers in context.

Resources
A set of loop cards as shown below. To order blank cards phone
01392 384697 and quote Devon County Council purchasing
catalogue number 78.2700.

Activity

✽ You need to write out the following numbers and sums on
each of 22 cards:

−8 ¦ −2 + 3	7 ¦ −4 − 2	−1 ¦ 7 − 5	4 ¦ 0 + −8	−6 ¦ 4 + −1
2 ¦ 2 − −5	9 ¦ 6 − −2	5 ¦ 12 − 3	0 ¦ 3 + 2	−9 ¦ −4 + 4
−4 ¦ 10 + −4	−10 ¦ −6 − 3	1 ¦ 5 − 15	−2 ¦ −3 + 7	−5 ¦ 5 − 7
3 ¦ 0 − 5	−3 ¦ 4 + −5	−7 ¦ 3 + 7	8 ¦ −4 − 3	10 ¦ −2 − 2
11 ¦ −1 − 2	6 ¦ 7 − −4			

✽ Deal a card to each student, or pair of students.

✽ Start off by asking '100 − 99'. The student with '1' on the left
of their card stands up and calls out this answer. They then
read the sum that is on the right of their card, i.e. '5 − 15'.

✽ This continues until all 22 cards have been read out and
you are back to the beginning again.

✽ You could time the class to complete one round and aim to
beat the time at the end of the lesson.

Differentiation

✽ ⇑ Get students to design their own loop on a topic of your choice,
preferably on a computer – the best one can be put to the test
next lesson.

Hands up

Objective covered

Integers, powers and roots
Recognise and use multiples and factors (divisors).

Aim

To recognise and use the multiples of 3 and 5 in context.

Activity

❋ Start the class counting up from 1. All students should:

- put up their left hand for a multiple of 3
- put up their right hand for a multiple of 5
- put up both hands if the number is a multiple of both 3 and 5.

❋ See how far can they get without making a mistake.

❋ Alternatively, you could go around the class individually.

Answer

1, 2, 3(L), 4, 5(R), 6(L), 7, 8, 9(L), 10(R), 11, 12(L), 13, 14, 15(LR), ...

Differentiation

❋ ⬆ Get students to say 'fizz' when they come to a multiple of 3, 'buzz' for a multiple of 5, and 'fizz-buzz' for both.

Odd one out

Objectives covered

Integers, powers and roots
Recognise and use multiples; use simple tests of divisibility.
Recognise squares of numbers.

Aim

To recognise multiples of 3 and 5 and square numbers up to 100.
To apply simple tests of divisibility as well as practising substituting
numbers into simple expressions.

Resources

100 grid for each student. To order a pack of thirty-five 100 grids (A6,
laminated and double sided), phone 01392 384697 and quote Devon
County Council purchasing catalogue number 45.5589.

Activity

⊛ Ask students to cross off the following list of numbers
from their 100 grid:

- all square numbers
- all numbers divisible by 3 or 'the multiples of 3'
- all numbers where the second digit is greater than or
  equal to the first
- all those divisible by 5 or 'the multiples of 5'
- all integers between 50 and 80 inclusive
- all those whose sum of the digits is divisible by 2
- all those numbers that satisfy $10n + 7$, when n is an
  integer between 0 and 9 inclusive.

⊛ The first student to call out the smallest remaining
number is the winner.

Answer

32

Differentiation

⊛ ⇑ Get students to make a set of clues for the class.

⊛ ⇓ Give the last set of numbers as 7, 17, 27, ... as
opposed to using the expression.

Multiple madness

Objective covered

Integers, powers and roots
Use simple tests of divisibility.

Aim

To understand place value and be confident in reading large numbers and using simple tests of divisibility.

Activity

- Get students to write the numbers 1 to 10 in a line in any order, for example, 13 524 769 810.

- Ask someone to read out their resulting number, in this case 'thirteen billion, five hundred and twenty-four million, seven hundred and sixty-nine thousand, eight hundred and ten'.

- Then ask a variety of questions such as:

  1 Is it a multiple of 10?

  2 Is it divisible by 3?

  3 Is it divisible by 2?

Answers

1 For the above example, yes.
2 No, the sum of the digits is 46 which subsequently add up to 10, so the number is not divisible by 3.
3 Yes, it's an even number.

Differentiation

- ⬆ Incorporate other tests of divisibility.

- ⬇ Get students to practise rounding their resulting number (to the nearest 10, 100 and 1000).

Asian square roots

Objective covered

Integers, powers and roots
Recognise squares of numbers to at least 12 × 12 and the corresponding roots.

Aim

To calculate square roots without a calculator by subtracting odd numbers.

Activity

- Introduce the ancient Asian method for finding square roots by using the example of $\sqrt{25}$.

- Firstly, get students to subtract the odd numbers 1, 3, 5, 7, … in turn from 25, until they reach zero.

- Then get them to count the number of subtractions they've done.

- This gives them the square root. In the case of $\sqrt{25}$:

  $25 - \mathbf{1} = 24$

  $24 - \mathbf{3} = 21$

  $21 - \mathbf{5} = 16$

  $16 - \mathbf{7} = 9$

  $9 - \mathbf{9} = 0$

  5 subtractions were needed, so $\sqrt{25} = 5$.

- Get students to find, using the same method:

  1 $\sqrt{16}$　　2 $\sqrt{49}$　　3 $\sqrt{64}$　　4 $\sqrt{169}$　　5 $\sqrt{121}$

Answers

1 　4　　　2 　7　　　3 　8　　　4 　13　　　5 　11

Differentiation

- ⬆ Discuss that the square root of a number could also be negative, for example, $\sqrt{25} = -5$ or 5.

Dry sponge competition

Objectives covered
Integers, powers and roots
Add, subtract, multiply and divide integers.
Use squares and cubes.

Aim
To practise mental methods of adding, subtracting and multiplying integers as well as using squares.

Resources
Most effective with a giant coloured sponge die. To order, phone 01392 384697 and quote Devon County Council purchasing catalogue number H 71.4950, for a foam cube with dimensions of 155 mm.

Activity

- ✸ Choose a rule, such as 'double the number caught' and then throw the sponge to a student.

- ✸ The student then doubles the number on the top face and throws the sponge back to you.

- ✸ The game continues and succeeds in keeping all students alert!

- ✸ For variety, you can change the rule as the game continues. Here are six examples:
  - double and add 1
  - square it and add 2
  - multiply by 3
  - add 11
  - minus 10
  - divide by 10.

Differentiation

- ✸ ⬆ Split the class into 2 teams and see how many dice they can return to you in, say, 1 minute, using the formula $d^2 + 3$ ('d' representing the number on the die).

Mathematical jumble

Objective covered

Integers, powers and roots
Recognise and use factors (divisors).

Aim

To practise recognising and using factors in context.

Activity

❋ Think of a sentence or word, for example 'Have a great Easter'.

❋ Re-write it in rows as opposed to one line (each row having the same number of letters), for example in 4 rows of 4:

```
H A V E
A G R E
A T E A
S T E R
```

❋ Then write down the letters as they are read vertically and ask students to un-jumble it.

❋ Examples you could use are:

1   HAASAGTTVREEEEAR

2   MASATETIAHCSESYMI!

3   NLGTSMOOUIUETNNLMR

Answers

1 HAVE A GREAT EASTER
2 MATHEMATICS IS EASY!

3 rows of 6:
```
M A T H E M
A T I C S I
S E A S Y !
```

3 NOT LONG UNTIL SUMMER

6 rows of 3:
```
N O T
L O N
G U N
T I L
S U M
M E R
```

Differentiation

❋ ⬆ Choose a longer sentence or a word where the number of letters has many factors. It will be harder for students to decipher!

Factor game

Objective covered/aim

Integers, powers and roots
Recognise and use factors (divisors) and common factor.

Resources

One ordinary die. Most effective with a giant coloured sponge die. To order, phone 01392 384697 and quote Devon County Council purchasing catalogue number H 71.4950, for a foam cube with dimensions of 155 mm.

Activity

⊛ Draw this grid on the board for students to copy.

	5	15	36
12			
4			
8			

⊛ The die is thrown and students put the number rolled in any one of the 9 cells.

⊛ The aim is to position each number so that it is a factor of at least one, and ideally both, of the outside numbers in the same row or column.

⊛ Students win 0, 1 or 2 points per cell, depending whether the number in that cell is a factor of 0, 1 or 2 of the corresponding outside numbers.

⊛ Get the class to add up their individual scores at the end – the highest score wins.

Answer

For the following grid, students would score 10 points:

	5	15	36
12	5	1	6
4	3	2	4
8	2	3	5

5 (1 pt), 1 (2 pt), 6 (2 pt), 3 (0 pt), 2 (1 pt)
4 (2 pt), 2 (1 pt), 3 (1 pt), 5 (0 pt)

Differentiation

⊛ ⇑ Use larger numbers around the outside.

Wordy maths

Objectives covered/aims

Integers, powers and roots
Recognise and use multiples, factors (divisors), triangular numbers and primes.
Use squares and cubes.

Activity

⚙ Copy this 4 by 4 grid on to the board:

Square number	Prime number	Multiple of 5	Even number
Multiple of 10	Multiple of 3	Ends in 1	Triangular number
Greater than 120	3-digit number	Odd	Factor of 30
Between 60 and 70	Cube number	Less than 5	First digit 2

⚙ Ask students to fill in their own 4 by 4 grid with a relevant number in each square, for example, they could have 9, 2, 10, 20 in the top row and so on.

⚙ Get students in turn to call out a number of their choice. Everyone who has that number crosses it off their grid.

⚙ Any students who have more than one of the number called, may cross them all off.

⚙ The first student to cross off all their numbers wins.

Differentiation

⚙ ⬇ Decrease the grid size to 3 by 3 and use only the more basic types of number.

⚙ ⬆ Increase the grid size to 5 by 5.

⚙ ⬆ Include Fibonacci numbers and powers.

Pair up

Objective covered

Integers, powers and roots
Use squares, positive and negative square roots, cubes and cube roots, and index notation for small positive integer powers.

Aim

To practise recognising mathematical connections between numbers, including the outcome of squaring and cubing numbers.

Activity

⚙ Quickly write on the board a variety of numbers such as:

$$125$$
$$16 \qquad\qquad 5$$
$$4$$
$$7 \qquad\qquad 3$$

⚙ How many different connections can students make between two or more of the numbers shown in, say, 3 minutes?

⚙ When the time is up, students need to come up to the board or discuss what links they can make between the numbers. For example, $4^2 = 16$, $5^3 = 125$, $7 - 3 = 4$, $(4 \times 3) - 7 = 5$, $16 - 7 - 4 = 5$, $\sqrt[3]{125} + 5 - 3 = 7$.

Differentiation

⚙ ⬆ ⬇ Use a variety of numbers to suit the ability range.

⚙ ⬆ Discuss BODMAS and the importance of brackets.

Around the world

Objective covered

Integers, powers and roots
Use index notation for integer powers and simple instances of the index laws.

Aim

To practise the index laws for multiplication and division of positive integer powers as well as practising rounding numbers to the nearest 1, 2 and 3 decimal places.

Activity

* Students must sit in pairs. Ask the first pair of students a question. The first to answer it correctly moves to join the next pair of students in the class.

* There are now three students competing and the first to get the next question right, moves on.

* If the student who joined the pair doesn't get the question right, they sit in the seat of the student who moves on.

* The student who has moved the most number of seats in, say, 10 minutes is the winner. Alternatively, instead of setting a time limit, you could go round the class twice, so that everyone gets two chances.

* Examples of questions you could use are:

1 2^3	2 3^0	3 $4^{\frac{1}{2}}$	4 $x^4 \times x^5$
5 $x^3 \times x^6$	6 $x^5 \div x^2$	7 $x^8 \div x^4$	8 $x^5 \div x^5$
9 Round 3.15 to 1 d.p.		10 Round 1.234 to 2 d.p.	

Answers

1 8	2 1	3 2 or −2	4 x^9	5 x^9
6 x^3	7 x^4	8 1 (x^0)	9 3.2	10 1.23

Differentiation

* ⬇ Change the topic to times tables, for example.

33

Powerful powers

Objective covered

Integers, powers and roots
Use index notation for integer powers and simple instances of the index laws.

Aim

To practise using index notation for integer powers and use the index laws for multiplication and division of positive integer powers.

Activity

⊛ Get students to discuss the following statement:

$$2^2 \times 2^3 = 2^5 \text{ therefore } 2^2 \times 3^2 = 6^4$$

⊛ Ask the following questions:

- Is the statement correct? If not, why not?
- Can you prove that it's wrong?
- What are the rules of indices?

⊛ Get students to answer these, leaving their answers in index form.

1 $3^8 \div 3^5$	2 $4^5 \div 4^2$	3 $2^5 \div 3^2$
4 $4^2 \times 4^3$	5 $5^5 \times 5^0$	6 $a^b \times a^c$
7 $a^d \div a^e$	8 $a^4 \times b^2$	

Answers

⊛ The statement is false. The index laws only work for powers of the same base number.
$2^2 \times 3^2 = 4 \times 9 = 36$, but $6^4 = 1296$.

⊛ When multiplying powers of the same number, you add the powers. When dividing powers of the same number, you subtract the powers.

1 3^3 2 4^3 3 Cannot be simplified   4 4^5
5 5^5 6 a^{b+c} 7 a^{d-e} 8 Cannot be simplified

The index link

Objective covered

Integers, powers and roots
Use index notation for integer powers and simple instances of the index laws.

Aim

To practise using index notation for integer
powers and simple instances of the index laws.

Resources

Individual whiteboards and pens (optional). To order a pack
of six dry-wipe whiteboards from Hope Education, Maths
supplies for secondary schools, phone 08451 202055 and
quote SM010/200 (A4) or SP001/200 (A3).

Activity

- Explain to the class that they are going to ask each other
  questions specific to the index laws, for example, x^0,
  $x^5 \div x^2$ or $x^3 \times y^4$.

- You direct the first question to the first two students of
  your choice, e.g. $x^{10} \times x^2$.

- The two students race to answer the question. The first to
  answer correctly should stand up and remain standing.
  This student then gives a new question to the next pair of
  students by writing it on their whiteboard.

- Once they've gone around the class once, half the
  students should be standing.

- Get students who are sitting down to ask a pair of
  standing students a question. The first to answer can
  remain standing, the other has to sit down.

- Continue in this way until there is only one student left
  standing. They are the winner.

Four in a line

Objective covered

Fractions, decimals, percentages, ratio and proportion
Identify equivalent fractions.

Aim

To practise converting between mixed and
improper fractions (mentally or otherwise).

Activity

⊛ Ask students to draw a 5 by 6 rectangle and fill it with
the numbers 3 to 32 (in any order).

⊛ Start putting mixed numbers in their simplest form on the
board, for example, $3\frac{3}{4}$. Students should cross the
numerator of the equivalent improper fraction off their
grid (for this example, they should cross off 15 because
3 ($\frac{3}{4} = \frac{15}{4}$).

⊛ The first student to cross off four in a line, with no gaps,
is the winner.

⊛ The following mixed numbers can be used to generate
all 30 numerators:

$2\frac{2}{5}$, $4\frac{1}{3}$, $3\frac{1}{3}$, $2\frac{2}{3}$, $2\frac{1}{4}$, $1\frac{1}{5}$, $5\frac{1}{5}$, $1\frac{1}{6}$, $2\frac{1}{2}$, $6\frac{1}{4}$, $7\frac{2}{3}$, $1\frac{1}{3}$, $4\frac{2}{3}$, $6\frac{2}{3}$, $4\frac{4}{5}$, $3\frac{3}{4}$,
$2\frac{1}{8}$, $2\frac{2}{7}$, $1\frac{1}{2}$, $3\frac{3}{5}$, $5\frac{3}{5}$, $4\frac{2}{5}$, $5\frac{4}{5}$, $3\frac{4}{5}$, $4\frac{1}{5}$, $7\frac{3}{4}$, $4\frac{2}{7}$, $10\frac{2}{3}$, $5\frac{2}{5}$, $1\frac{5}{6}$

Answers

For the mixed numbers given above, students should cross off:
12, 13, 10, 8, 9, 6, 26, 7, 5, 25, 23, 4, 14, 20, 24, 15,
17, 16, 3, 18, 28, 22, 29, 19, 21, 31, 30, 32, 27, 11

Differentiation

⊛ ⇓ A smaller grid size could be used.

⊛ ⇑ Students could take turns reading out mixed numbers of their
choice.

Mystery number

Objective covered

Fractions, decimals, percentages, ratio and proportion
Multiply an integer by a fraction.

Aim

To practise calculating fractions of quantities.

Activity

❀ Draw this on the board:

3	6	4

❀ Pose the problem:

'One of these numbers is half my mystery number,
one is a quarter of it and the other is a third.
What is my mystery number?'

❀ Repeat, using 9 12 18 .

Answer

12 for the first set.
36 for the second set.

Differentiation

❀ ⬆ Invite students to come up with an alternative mystery number
puzzle for the class to decipher.

❀ ⬆ Discuss factors: 3, 4 and 6 are all factors of 12.

Strategies

Objective covered/aim

Fractions, decimals, percentages, ratio and proportion
*Calculate percentages and fractions of quantities and find
the outcome of a given percentage increase or decrease.*

Activity

✦ Ask students to discuss how they would work out the
following without a calculator:

1 What is $\frac{1}{32}$ as a
percentage?

2 What is 75% of 30
euros?

3 What is 40% of $400?

4 What is 125% of 240?

5 Increase 480 m by 20%.

6 What is $\frac{4}{5}$ of 20?

7 What is $1\frac{1}{2}$ of 18?

8 Given that 38^2 is 1444,
what is 3.8^2?

Answers

Ideas for discussion:

1 $\frac{1}{4} = 25\%$, so $\frac{1}{8} = 12.5\%$, $\frac{1}{16} = 6.25\%$ and $\frac{1}{32} = 3.125\%$.

2 50% of 30 is 15, so 25% is 7.5 and 75% is 15 + 7.5 = 22.5 euros.

3 10% of $400 is 40, so 40% is 40 × 4 = $160.

4 25% of 240 = $\frac{1}{2}$ of 120 = 60, so 125% is 240 + 60 = 300.

5 To find 20%, divide 480 m by 10 then times by 2 to get 96 m.
Add this to 480 m to get 576 m. Alternatively, 20% can be found
by dividing by 5.

6 $\frac{1}{5}$ of 20 is 4, so $\frac{4}{5}$ is 4 × 4 = 16.

7 $\frac{1}{2}$ of 18 is 9, so $1\frac{1}{2}$ of 18 is 18 + 9 = 27.

8 3.8 is $\frac{1}{10}$ of 38, so 3.8^2 is $\frac{1}{10^2}$ of 38^2, which is 14.44. (You could
demonstrate this using easier numbers, such as 100^2 and 10^2.
Remind students that they can check the answer is the right size
using estimation.)

Trick with 11s

Objective covered

Number operations and the relationships between them
Understand multiplication as it applies to whole numbers;
know how to use the laws of arithmetic.

Aim

To practise using the laws of arithmetic to multiply integers
effectively whilst also practising mental methods of calculation.

Activity

⊛ See if students can spot the trick for multiplying by 11
   (other than multiplying by 10 and adding on):
   $13 \times 11 = 143$
   $18 \times 11 = 198$
   $23 \times 11 = 253$
   $45 \times 11 = 495$

⊛ Ask students to use the trick to find 33×11.

Answers

The two digits of the number being multiplied by 11 become the first
and last digits of the answer. The middle digit of the answer is the sum
of the outer digits. For example, the outer digits for 13×11 are 1 and
3, and the middle digit is $1 + 3 = 4$.
$33 \times 11 = 363$

Differentiation

⊛ ⇑ Pose the question 'What happens if you have to multiply 88 by
   11?' (It still works, you just have to carry the tens digit from 16
   over to give the answer 968.)

⊛ ⇑ See if students can prove why this trick works.

Double and half

Objective covered

Number operations and the relationships between them
Understand multiplication and division as they apply to whole numbers and decimals.

Aim

To practise using the laws of arithmetic to multiply integers and decimals effectively whilst also practising mental methods of calculation.

Resources

Individual whiteboards and pens. To order a pack of six dry-wipe whiteboards from Hope Education, Maths supplies for secondary schools, phone 08451 202055 and quote SM010/200 (A4) or SP001/200 (A3).

Activity

⊛ Ask students to discuss how they could do the following in their heads:

$18 \times 6 (= 9 \times 12 = 108)$ $6 \times 4.5 (= 3 \times 9 = 27)$
$12 \times 7.5 (= 6 \times 15 = 3 \times 30 = 90)$

⊛ Ask students to get into teams and give each team a whiteboard to write answers on.

⊛ Introduce a points system: 10 points for the first team to give the correct answer, 5 points for the second team. Reduce these to 2 points for second attempts.

⊛ Ask questions like these:

1   24×2.5 2 14×3.5 3 16×4.5

4   22×5.5 5 22×6.5

⊛ It may be worthwhile keeping a tally of the team results on the board.

Answers

1   $12 \times 5 = 60$ 2 $7 \times 7 = 49$ 3 $8 \times 9 = 72$
4   $11 \times 11 = 121$ 5 $11 \times 13 = 143$

It's questionable

Objective covered

Number operations and the relationships between them
Know and use the order of operations, including brackets.

Aim

To practise using BODMAS for the order of operations, including brackets.

Activity

⊛ Students need to decipher what the '?' represents in each of these sums, using their knowledge of BODMAS. They may only choose from the numbers 1, 2, 3, 4 and 5, and they may not repeat any of these numbers in each sum.

1 $? + ? - ? = 4$

2 $? \times ? - ? = 3$

3 $(? + ?) \div ? = 2$

4 $(? + ?) \div (? + ?) = 1$

Answers

Example solutions are given below. Others are also possible.

1 $5 + 1 - 2$ 2 $4 \times 2 - 5$ 3 $(5 + 3) \div 4$ 4 $(3 + 4) \div (2 + 5)$

Differentiation

⊛ ⬆ Ask this additional question:

5 $(\sqrt{?} + ?)^2 = 1$

Answer: $(\sqrt{4} + 3)^2 = 1$, since $(-2 + 3)^2 = 1$. Explain to students that a square root can be negative.

⊛ ⬆ You could use different letters instead of question marks.

⊛ ⬆ The students could design their own question for the class.

Dice countdown

Objective covered

Number operations and the relationships between them
Use the order of operations, including brackets, with more complex calculations.

Aim

To practise using BODMAS for the order of operations, including brackets, as well as the skill of estimating.

Resources

One ordinary die. Most effective with a giant coloured sponge die. To order, phone 01392 384697 and quote Devon County Council purchasing catalogue number H 71.4950, for a foam cube with dimensions of 155 mm.

Activity

⊛ Set a target number such as 28.

⊛ Throw a die four times to get, for example, 3, 4, 2 and 6.

⊛ Students have 2 minutes to use these numbers and any operations to get as close to the target number as possible.

Answer

Possible answers are:
$(3 + 4) \times (6 - 2)$
$6^2 - 3 \times 4 + 2^2$
$4^2 + 2 \times 6$
Other answers are also possible.

Differentiation

⊛ ⬆ Use a differently numbered die and stress that all numbers must be used.

Four 4s

Objective covered

Number operations and the relationships between them
Use the order of operations, including brackets, with more complex calculations.

Aim

To practise using BODMAS for the order of operations, including brackets.

Activity

- Ask students to make each of the numbers 1 to 10 using four 4s and any operations. Encourage them to use the rules of BODMAS.

- See if students can find other ways to do it.

Answers

For example:

$4 \div 4 \times 4 \div 4 = 1 \times 1 = 1$

$4 \div 4 \times 4 \div \sqrt{4} = 1 \times 2 = 2$

$4 \div \sqrt{4} + 4 \div 4 = 2 + 1 = 3$

$4 \div \sqrt{4} + 4 \div \sqrt{4} = 2 + 2 = 4$

$4 + 4 \div \sqrt{4} \div \sqrt{4} = 4 + 2 \div 2 = 4 + 1 = 5$

$4 + 4 - (4 - \sqrt{4}) = 4 + 4 - 2 = 6$

$4 + 4 - 4 \div 4 = 4 + 4 - 1 = 7$

$4 + 4 + 4 - 4 = 8$

$4 + 4 + 4 \div 4 = 8 + 1 = 9$

$4 + 4 + (4 - \sqrt{4}) = 8 + 2 = 10$

Differentiation

- ⬆ Ask students to make up a similar problem, using a different number.

Working backwards

Objective covered

Number operations and the relationships between them
Use the order of operations, including brackets, with more complex calculations.

Aim

To practise using BODMAS for the order of operations, as well as estimation skills and using a calculator efficiently.

Activity

⊛ Give students these answers:

    1 58   2 56   3 746

⊛ Tell them that these are the answers to three questions, which each use all the numbers 25, 5, 6, 10 and 73 only once.

⊛ Students must work out what the questions could have been. They can use any operations as well as brackets, squaring and square rooting.

Answers

Example solutions are given below. Others are also possible.
1 $73 - 6 \times 5 + (25 - 10) = 58$ or $(73 - 25 + 10) \times (6 - 5)$
2 $73 + 6 - 25 + 10 \div 5 = 56$ or $73 - 6 - 10 - \sqrt{25} \div 5$
3 $73 \times 10 + \sqrt{25} + 5 + 6 = 746$ or $73 \times (\sqrt{25} + 5) + 10 + 6$

Differentiation

⊛ ⇑ Ask students to come up with their own backwards problems.

⊛ ⇑ Get students to check their answers on a calculator.

And the target number is ...

Objective covered
Number operations and the relationships between them
Use the order of operations.

Aim
To practise mental methods of calculation as well as encourage the use of BODMAS.

Resources
A rotating dice magimixer. To order, phone 01392 384697 and quote Devon County Council purchasing catalogue number ELEDT001, for a pack of five rotating dice magimixers.

Alternatively, use six ordinary dice and a die with faces numbered 10, 20, 30, 40, 50 and 60. To order a pack of ten 6-sided blank dice, phone 01392 384697 and quote Devon County Council purchasing catalogue number 78.2702.

Activity
- Keep the 'tens' die and one ordinary die separate from the rest.
- Roll these together to give the target number, by adding their scores.
- Roll the remaining five dice and write these numbers on the board.
- Each of these numbers must be used once only to produce the target number.
- Students may use any operation (+, −, ×, ÷).
- A small percentage may not work. Encourage students to discuss why. For examplek, if five 1s are thrown, no target number can be produced.

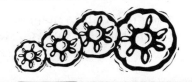

Very small but very important

Objective covered

Number operations and the relationships between them
Understand the effects of multiplying and dividing by numbers between 0 and 1.

Aim

To practise understanding the effects of multiplying and dividing by numbers between 0 and 1, and use this to help test the validity of answers.

Activity

⚙ Discuss what happens when integers are divided by very small numbers (between 0 and 1). For example:

$100 \div \frac{1}{2}$, $100 \div \frac{1}{5}$, $100 \div \frac{1}{10}$, $100 \div \frac{1}{1000}$.

⚙ Discuss what happens when integers are multiplied by very small numbers (between 0 and 1). For example:

$100 \times \frac{1}{2}$, $100 \times \frac{1}{20}$, $100 \times \frac{1}{200}$.

⚙ Give students some questions and answers, and ask them to discuss whether they are correct or not (without using a calculator).
For example:

$26 \times 0.65 = 16.9$ (Yes)
$214 \times 0.32 = 684.8$ (No, 68.48)
$123 \div 0.2 = 61.5$ (No, 615)

Answers

When **dividing** a positive number by a number less than one, the result will be a **larger** number than the one you started with.

When **multiplying** a positive number by a number less than one, the result will be a **smaller** number than the one you started with.

First to 100

Objective covered

Mental methods and rapid recall of number facts
Consolidate the rapid recall of number facts, including integer complements to 100.

Aim

To practise the rapid mental recall of number facts, including positive integer complements to 100.

Resources

Number fans (not essential but encourages a quieter lesson). To order a set of 0–9 petal-shaped number fans, phone 01392 384697 and quote Devon County Council purchasing catalogue number 45.5591.

Activity

⊛ Students use number fans or call out the number needed to make 100. For example:

- you shout 23, they shout 77
- you shout –10, they shout 110
- you shout 46, they shout 54.

Differentiation

⊛ ⬇ Ask students to make 10.

⊛ ⬆ Ask them to make 1000.

⊛ ⬆ Incorporate decimals and fractions, for example, $25\frac{1}{3}$ and $74\frac{2}{3}$ make 100.

301

Objective covered
Mental methods and rapid recall of number facts
Consolidate the rapid recall of number facts, including multiplication facts.

Aim
To practise the rapid mental recall of multiplication facts up to 6 × 6 and practise adding whole numbers.

Resources
An ordinary die for each student in the class.

Activity
- Competing against each other in pairs, students take turns rolling two dice together.
- They write down the two numbers and multiply them together, for example, 4 × 6 = 24.
- On their next turn, the result is added to their running total.
- The first student to get to exactly 301 wins.
- They may 'stick' if they roll the die and know the result will go over 301, but they lose their turn.

Differentiation
- ⬆ Use different dice, for example, ones numbered 1–8.
- ⬇ Use dice numbered 0–5 and get students to reach 101.

Times tables undercover

Objective covered

Mental methods and rapid recall of number facts
Consolidate the rapid recall of number facts, including multiplication facts to 10 × 10.

Aim

To practise the rapid mental recall of multiplication facts to 10 × 10, and to revise other mathematical facts and associated vocabulary.

Activity

⊛ Get each student to draw a 5 by 5 grid and fill it with the numbers 1 to 25 in any order.

⊛ Ask questions so that each student can cross off the answers from their grid.

⊛ The first to get five in a line wins.

⊛ The trick is to ask 'interesting' questions such as:

1 What is the total number of legs on 6 chickens?

2 What is the total number of hooves on 5 cows?

3 What is the number of letters in the capital of Italy multiplied by 4?

4 How many sides does a pentagon have?

5 What is the square root of the number of years in a century?

6 How many chairs are there in a hall if there are 5 rows of 5?

Answers

1 12   2 20   3 16 (Rome)   4 5   5 10   6 25

Differentiation

⊛ ⬆ Change the numbers entered into their grid.

Around the clock 1

Objective covered
Mental methods and rapid recall of number facts
Consolidate the rapid recall of number facts, including multiplication facts.

Aim
To practise the rapid mental recall of multiplication facts.

Activity

- ⊛ Put up on the board the multiples of a multiplication table you want to practise, for example, the 6 times table:

```
        48  36  42
    18   \  |  /   6
          \ | /
   24 ——( × 6 )—— 72
          / | \
    66   /  |  \   30
        54  12  60
```

- ⊛ Point at the end numbers and ask students to call out the number that 6 needs to be multiplied by to get that number. For example, if you point at '6', the class should call out '1'.

- ⊛ Go faster and faster as you rotate around the central number, trying to catch someone out, in which case, you start from the beginning again.

- ⊛ See how long it takes to get twice 'round the clock' with no mistakes.

Differentiation

- ⊛ ⬆ Choose an individual for the challenge and record the time it takes them to get, say, ten right.

- ⊛ ⬆ Get two students competing against one another.

Full house

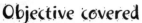

Objective covered

Mental methods and rapid recall of number facts
Consolidate the rapid recall of number facts, including multiplication facts to 10 × 10.

Aim

To practise the rapid mental recall of multiplication facts.

Activity

- ✸ Each student draws a large 3 by 3 grid and fills each cell with a different times table sum (specify which tables you want to include).

- ✸ Give the answer to a times table, for example, 12 (record it on a piece of paper to avoid repeats and to check that students have calculated it properly).

- ✸ In the case of 12, students could cross off 2 × 6 or 3 × 4.

- ✸ It may be worth telling them to lightly cross their sums off, so that they can still be read for checking.

- ✸ Allow students to cross off all the sums that fit the answer.

- ✸ The first student to cross all their sums off wins.

- ✸ Hopefully after a number of goes, they will see the benefit of choosing equivalent factor pairs.

Differentiation

- ✸ ⬇ Change the rules so that the first student to get 3 in a line wins (for speed).

- ✸ ⬆ Introduce factors and factor pairs as a discussion point.

- ✸ ⬆ Extend the times tables specified.

Make 10

Objective covered
Mental methods and rapid recall of number facts
Consolidate and extend mental methods of calculation to include decimals and fractions.

Aim
To practise adding fractions and decimals, and reading coordinates.

Resources
OHP and an OHT prepared as below. Cover the numbers inside the axes with interlocking cubes or counters.

4	7	5	$6\frac{1}{4}$	2
3	8	9.75	6	$3\frac{3}{4}$
2	5	0.25	9	9.5
1	1	4	3	0.5
0	1	2	3	4

Activity

⊛ Students (or teams) take turns to call out two pairs of coordinates, for example (4, 2) and (4, 1).

⊛ Reveal these hidden numbers as 9.5 and 0.5. Since these add to 10, the numbers are left revealed and the student (or team) may pick again having gained 1 point.

⊛ If subsequent chosen pairs of coordinates do not add to 10, the numbers are hidden again and it's the next student's (or team's) turn to pick.

⊛ The winner is the student or team to gain the most points.

Differentiation

⊛ ⬆ Use an alternative quadrant on the OHT.

Easy decimals

Objective covered
Mental methods and rapid recall of number facts
Consolidate and extend mental methods of calculation.

Aim
To interpret division as a multiplicative inverse and extend mental and written methods of calculation, by multiplying and dividing decimals.

Activity

✳ Discuss the method that has been used to answer the following divisions.

$0.48 \div 0.12 = 48 \div 12 = 4$

$0.10 \div 0.5 = 10 \div 50 = \frac{10}{50}$ or $\frac{1}{5}$ or $\frac{2}{10}$ or 0.2

$0.6 \div 0.02 = 60 \div 2 = 30$

✳ Get the class to try these questions and then check their answers on a calculator:

1    $0.36 \div 0.12$ 2 $3.5 \div 0.5$ 3 $0.8 \div 0.02$

✳ Ask students if they think the same method could be used for multiplying decimals. Write some examples on the board:

$0.3 \times 0.2 = 3 \times 2 = 6$ $0.5 \times 0.5 = 25$

Demonstrate that these are incorrect by asking a student to work out the correct answers on their calculator (0.06, 0.25).

✳ Discuss why the method doesn't work for multiplication and the methods that could be used instead.

Answers

1 3   2 7   3 $80 \div 2 = 40$

Methods that could be used for multiplication are:

- Look at how many digits are after the points in the question and make sure there are the same number in the answer, for example '0.3 × 0.2' has 2 numbers after the points, so the answer is 0.06.

- Convert the decimals to fractions: $0.3 \times 0.2 = \frac{3}{10} \times \frac{2}{10} = \frac{6}{100} = 0.06$.

Around the clock 2

Objective covered
Mental methods and rapid recall of number facts
Consolidate and extend mental methods of calculation.

Aim
To practise mental methods of calculation, working with fractions, percentages, factors and powers.

Activity

⊛ Put on the board the number 40 surrounded by various fractions, percentages, factors and powers:

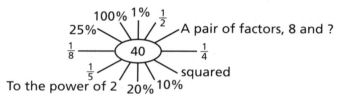

⊛ As you point at the end numbers students must call out the answer. For example, if you point at 25%, the class should call out '10', since 25% of 40 is 10.

⊛ Go faster and faster as you rotate around the central number, trying to catch someone out, in which case, you start from the beginning again.

⊛ See how long it takes to get twice 'round the clock' with no mistakes.

Differentiation

⊛ ⬆⬇ Adapt the activity by using a different central number.

⊛ ⬆ Choose an individual for the challenge and record the time it takes them to get, say, 10 right.

⊛ ⬆ Get two students competing against one another.

⊛ ⬆ Get students to design their own question, including squares, cubes and roots.

Blast off

YEAR 8

Objective covered
Mental methods and rapid recall of number facts
Consolidate and extend mental methods of calculation.

Aim
To consolidate the rapid recall of number facts such as squares and square roots as well as using conventional 2-D coordinates.

Activity

- ✹ Draw on the board x- and y-axes from 0 to 3 and secretly write the coordinates of where the 'rocket' is on a piece of paper, for example (2, 3).

- ✹ You should have ready a list of questions that go with each coordinate, for example:

(0, 0) 7×8 (= 56)	(2, 0) $\sqrt{81}$ (= 9 or –9)
(0, 1) 6×9 (= 54)	(2, 1) $\sqrt{100}$ (= 10 or –10)
(0, 2) 5×7 (= 35)	(2, 2) $100 - 32$ (= 68)
(0, 3) 100×100 (= 10 000)	**(2, 3) $1\,000\,000 - 1$ (= 999 999)**
(1, 0) 7×7 (= 49)	(3, 0) $93 + 12$ (= 105)
(1, 1) 8×8 (= 64)	(3, 1) $? \times 8 = 24$ (3)
(1, 2) 0×4 (= 0)	(3, 2) $?^2 = 36$ (6)
(1, 3) $\sqrt{64}$ (= 8 or –8)	(3, 3) 50×0 (= 0)

- ✹ Students take turns in stating coordinates and then answering the associated question.

- ✹ If they get the answer right, you tell the class if the rocket is there or not.

- ✹ If they get the answer wrong, you don't reveal anything and they lose a life.

- ✹ The class has five lives until blast off!

Differentiation

- ✹ ⬆ ⬇ Change the questions to a topic of your choice and/or the number of lives allowed.

Number register

Objective covered

Mental methods and rapid recall of number facts
Extend mental methods of calculation, working with decimals, fractions, percentages, factors, powers and roots.

Aim

To practise mental methods and rapid recall of number facts on a topic of your choice.

Activity

❀ Practise work with decimals, fractions, percentages, factors, powers and roots by asking students a quick question after their name as you call out the register. For example:
'Anbany: What is half of 0.5 as a decimal?' (0.25)
'Barnes: What is half of 0.25 as a fraction?' ($\frac{1}{8}$)
'Charles: What is 20% of 200?' (40)
'Daw: What is 2^3?' (8)

❀ How many questions can they correctly answer in a row?

Differentiation

❀ ⬇ Ask students to call out the multiples of, say, 5.

❀ ⬆ Each student, in turn, could ask the next student in the register a question.

Estimation golf

Objective covered
Mental methods and rapid recall of number facts
Make and justify estimates and approximations of calculations.

Aim
To practise approximating and justifying estimates for calculations given to 1 decimal place.

Activity
- ⚙ Divide the class into two or more teams.
- ⚙ Then, on the board, write a sum, for example, $\sqrt{38}$.
- ⚙ Each team then has to estimate the answer to 1 decimal place.
- ⚙ If the team gets it spot-on, it's a 'hole in one' and they score 10 points.
- ⚙ If neither team gets it, they can have a second attempt and try and get a 'birdie' for 5 points.
- ⚙ The team with the most points wins.
- ⚙ Ideas for sums are:

  1 $\sqrt{38}$

  2 $26 \div 15$

  3 14.3% of 89

  4 $\sqrt{50}$

  5 12% of 62

Answers
1 6.2 2 1.7 3 12.7 4 7.1 5 7.4

Differentiation
- ⚙ ⬆ Get students to guess the number to 2 decimal places.
- ⚙ ⬇ Get students to estimate the answer to the nearest whole number.

Max subtract

Objective covered
Written methods
Use standard column procedures to subtract whole numbers.

Aim
To practise using standard written column procedures to subtract whole numbers.

Resources
Most effective with a giant coloured sponge die. To order, phone 01392 384697 and quote Devon County Council purchasing catalogue number H 71.4950, for a foam cube with dimensions of 155 mm.

Activity

⊛ Students need to draw two rows of four boxes and enter a '7' in the top-left box (to avoid getting negatives).

$$\boxed{7}\ \square\ \square\ \square$$
$$-\ \square\ \square\ \square\ \square$$

⊛ The die is then rolled seven times and everyone fills the number rolled, into one of their remaining seven boxes.

⊛ The aim is to get the largest possible number when the bottom row is subtracted from the top.

⊛ You could introduce a points system whereby they gain 10 points if they get the largest number possible and 5 points if they get more than you do on the board!

Differentiation

⊛ ⇑ Omit the initial 7 and see if students can work with negative numbers to obtain the smallest number possible.

Upside down calculator

Objective covered

Calculator methods
Enter numbers and interpret the display.

Aim

To enter numbers into a calculator and interpret the display in an unconventional and fun way.

Resources

Calculators. Individual whiteboards and pens (optional). To order a pack of six dry-wipe whiteboards from Hope Education, Maths supplies for secondary schools, phone 08451 202055 and quote SM010/200 (A4) or SP001/200 (A3).

Activity

⊛ Get students to type in the number 7735 and turn the calculator upside down to read the word SELL.

⊛ Read out these numbers to see if they can decipher the words on the calculator:

| 1 | 5537 | 2 | 5317 | 3 | 55 178 |

⊛ Next read out these words to see if they can work out the number to input:

| 4 | BELL | 5 | BLESS | 6 | SLOB | 7 | LOO |
| 8 | LOBES | 9 | SOB | 10 | BOILS | | |

Answers

1	LESS	2	LIES	3	BLISS	
4	7738	5	55 378	6	8075	7	0.07
8	53 807	9	805	10	57 108	

Differentiation

⊛ ⬇ Get students to work in pairs and put their answers on a whiteboard. Then ask everyone to hold up their whiteboards at the same time to see who's out of the next round.

Calculator race

Objective covered

Calculator methods
Use the constant, sign change keys, function keys for powers, roots and fractions, brackets and the memory; use the reciprocal key.

Aim

To practise carrying out calculations effectively and efficiently using a calculator as well as to practise rounding numbers to a number of decimal places and significant figures and introduce 'reciprocal'.

Resources

Scientific calculators.

Activity

❀ Students race to give the correct answer from their calculator display (read correctly), for the following sums:

1 2^{18}

2 $\sqrt[3]{189}$ to 1 d.p.

3 $\frac{2}{7} + \frac{1}{5}$ in its simplest form as a fraction and a decimal to 2 d.p.

4 $1\frac{1}{8} + 2\frac{3}{5}$ in its simplest form as a fraction and a decimal to 2 d.p.

5 $(14 + \sqrt{83}) - (112 - 2^5)$

6 the reciprocal of 8.

❀ Encourage the use of the $\boxed{a^{b}/_{c}}$ button for questions 3 and 4.

Answers

1 262 144
2 5.7
3 $\frac{17}{35}$ and 0.49
4 $3\frac{29}{40}$ and 3.73
5 −57
6 0.125

Differentiation

❀ ⬇ Concentrate on one topic, such as calculating fractions using the $\boxed{a^{b}/_{c}}$ button.

❀ ⬇ Discuss what happens if you leave the brackets out of calculation 5. Refer to an easier example, such as $(1 + 2) - (3 + 4)$ versus $1 + 2 - 3 + 4$.

Standard problem

YEAR 9

Objective covered
Calculator methods
Enter numbers and interpret the display in context (numbers in standard form).

Aim
To practise interpreting the calculator display when it appears in standard form and begin writing numbers in standard form.

Resources
Scientific calculators.

Activity

 Ask the class to use their calculators, with room in the display for only 10 digits, to work out:

1   123 456 × 7 891 011

2   345 678 × 2 323 232

3   1.234 56 ÷ 7 891 011

4   0.004 56 ÷ 45

Make sure students are able to interpret the display as an ordinary number and as a number written in standard form.

Answers
1 974 192 654 000 or 9.74×10^{11} to 3 s.f.
2 803 090 191 300 or 8.03×10^{11} to 3 s.f.
3 0.000 000 156 451 435 7 or 1.56×10^{-7} to 3 s.f.
4 0.000 101 333 333 3 or 1.01×10^{-4} to 3 s.f.

Subs 1

Objective covered

Equations, formulae and identities
Use simple formulae from mathematics and other subjects; substitute positive integers into simple linear expressions and formulae.

Aim

To practise substituting integers into simple formulae.

Resources

Number fans. To order a set of 0–9 petal-shaped number fans, phone 01392 384697 and quote Devon County Council purchasing catalogue number 45.5591.

Activity

✳ Write four letters on the board with their values, for example, $a = 3$, $b = 4$, $c = 5$ and $d = 10$. (Alternatively, ask students to write their own choice of four numbers, then assign a letter to each.)

✳ Ask the class, as individuals or in pairs, to use their number fans to find the value of, say:

1	$2a$	2	$3c$	3	$5d$	4	$3c + 2$
5	$4b + 5$	6	$2c + 3a$	7	$3ab$	8	$2bd$
9	$d \div c$	10	$\frac{c}{d}$				

Answers

1	6	2	15	3	50	4	17
5	21	6	19	7	36	8	80
9	2	10	$\frac{1}{2}$				

Hidden rule

Objective covered/aim

Equations, formulae and identities
Use simple formulae from mathematics and other subjects.

Activity

⊛ Draw the following grid on the board, but NOT the numbers in brackets (these are the answers). You could use a red for the nine numbers in the centre and blue for ⑤, ⑫ and ⑬.

(10)	(9)	(10)	(9)	⑤
(10)	4	2	3	(11)
(9)	5	2	2	⑫
⑬	1	4	3	(7)
(7)	(21)	(8)	(9)	(11)

⊛ Students must discover the rule, using the three answers given. They must then use the rule to fill in the rest of the answers around the edges of the grid.

⊛ Explain to students that each outer (blue) number is made by substituting the three inner (red) numbers in the same row, column or diagonal into the same formula.

Answer

The rule is:
'Multiply the two further numbers on the line, then add the closest.'
For example:
$1 \times 2 + 3 = 5$
$5 \times 2 + 2 = 12$
$3 \times 4 + 1 = 13$

Differentiation

⊛ ⬆ Use a more complicated rule as an extension.

⊛ ⬇ Give a simple rule for the less able, such as 'add all three numbers'.

Numbered words

Objective covered
Equations, formulae and identities
Substitute positive integers.

Aim
To appreciate that different letters can be used to represent different numbers.

Activity
✤ Ask students to imagine that A = 1, B = 2, C = 3, D = 4, E = 5, F = 6, G = 7, H = 8 and I = 9, then ask them to say what words these numbers spell out:

1　85

2　214

3　312

4　2514

5　8945

✤ Ensure that students realise, at this stage, that letters are rarely worth these convenient values.

Answers
1 HE　　2 BAD　　3 CAB　　4 BEAD　　5 HIDE

Differentiation
✤ ⬆ Get students to come up with their own number system and corresponding word.

Missing letters

Objective covered

Equations, formulae and identities
*Know that algebraic operations follow the same
conventions and order as arithmetic operations.*

Aim

To practise manipulating or transforming
algebraic expressions.

Activity

⊛ Draw this grid on the board for students to copy.

+	?	?
?	$5x + 4y$	$2x + 3y$
?	$6x + 5y$	$3x + 4y$

⊛ Students must work out what algebraic expression each '?'
could be.

⊛ Ask them to find as many other ways to solve the grid as
possible.

Answers

This is one of an infinite number of possible solutions. To generate
others, add any quantity of x or y to both column headings and
subtract the same quantity from both row headings.

+	$5x + y$	$2x$
$3y$	$5x + 4y$	$2x + 3y$
$x + 4y$	$6x + 5y$	$3x + 4y$

Differentiation

⊛ ⬆ Students could try and make a grid of their own for the class to solve.

Algebra grid

Objective covered

Equations, formulae and identities
Use formulae from mathematics and other subjects; substitute integers into simple formulae.

Aim

To practise substituting integers into simple formulae and then expressions involving small powers.

Activity

❀ Draw this grid on the board for students to copy.

	4	5	2
4			
5			
3			

❀ Tell students that the numbers at the top are values of a and the numbers down the left-hand side are values of b.

❀ Write a formula on the board, for example, $3a + b$.

❀ Students must fill in the 3 by 3 grid as fast as they can.

Answer

	4	5	2
4	16	19	10
5	17	20	11
3	15	18	9

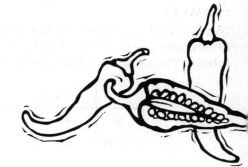

Differentiation

❀ ⇑ You could change the formula to, for example, $3a^2 + 4b$. You could also change the values of a and b.

Subs 2

Objective covered

Equations, formulae and identities
Use formulae from mathematics and other subjects;
substitute integers into simple formulae.

Aim

To practise substituting integers into simple formulae and expressions involving small powers.

Resources

Number fans. To order a set of 0–9 petal-shaped number fans, phone 01392 384697 and quote Devon County Council purchasing catalogue number 45.5591.

Activity

⚙ Write four letters on the board with their values, for example, $a = -1$, $b = 2$, $c = -4$ and $d = 10$. (Alternatively, ask students to write their own choice of four numbers, then assign a letter to each.)

⚙ Ask the class to use their number fans to find the value of, say:

1 a^2	2 b^2	3 $2c^2$	4 $b^2 + c$
5 abc	6 $2d + 3c$	7 $\frac{d}{b}$	8 $b^3 - a$
9 b^2c^2	10 $(2c)^2$		

Answers

1 1	2 4	3 32	4 0
5 8	6 8	7 5	8 9
9 64	10 64		

Equal 20

Objective covered

Equations, formulae and identities
*Use formulae from mathematics and other subjects;
substitute integers into simple formulae.*

Aim

To practise substituting integers into expressions and formulae.

Resources

Individual whiteboards and pens. To order a pack of 6 dry-wipe whiteboards from Hope Education, Maths supplies for secondary schools, phone 08451 202055 and quote SM010/200 (A4) or SP001/200 (A3).

Activity

⊛ Write four letters on the board with their values, for example, $a = 3$, $b = 4$, $c = 5$ and $d = 10$. (Alternatively, ask students to write their own choice of four numbers, then assign a letter to each.)

⊛ See how many equations the class can come up with, using the letters on the board, to give an answer of 20.

Answers

Some possible answers are:
$2c + d = 20$
$bc = 20$
$c^2 - c = 20$
$3c + d - c = 20$

Differentiation

⊛ ⬆ Ask a student to come up with a different target number and see who can produce most equations.

Inequality match

Objective covered / aim
Equations, formulae and identities
Solve linear inequalities in one variable, and represent the solution set on a number line.

Resources
A pack of blank cards. To order a pack of 200 blank cards, phone 01392 384697 and quote Devon County Council purchasing catalogue number 78.2700.

Activity

⊛ Give each student a blank card. Go round the class, telling each pair of students to draw either a number line or a graphical region on one of their blank cards and the matching inequality that you specify on the other blank card. Give a different inequality to each pair. For example, you may ask one pair to draw:

$$x \geqslant 1$$

⊛ Where graphical regions are displayed students must shade the unwanted region to show the solution to the inequality, so that their cards make a pair.

⊛ Write all the inequalities on the board.

⊛ Circulate and check that all the drawings are correct, or ask students to check each other's work.

⊛ Collect all the cards in, shuffle them and then deal one to each student again.

⊛ Each student now has to find their partner, as quickly as possible.

Differentiation

⊛ ⇓ You could prepare the cards beforehand.

⊛ ⇑ Ask more able students to draw more complex inequalities in one variable, such as $2 \leqslant x < 3$ or $3 < 3x \leqslant 9$.

Unusual coding

Objective covered

Equations, formulae and identities
Use formulae from mathematics and other subjects; substitute numbers into expressions and formulae.

Aim

To practise substituting integers into expressions, including those with powers and roots.

Activity

- ✺ Write A = 1, B = 2, C = 3, D = 4, etc. on the board.

- ✺ Explain to students that they are going to substitute these values into a series of expressions, to give a series of digits. Each digit must then be replaced with its letter equivalent to find a word.

- ✺ Ask students to work out the following words:

    1 $(J + C)$ (A) $(V - B)$ $(D \times B)$ $(X - E)$

    2 $(C + D + L)$ $(3E)$ $(2F)$ (B^2)

    3 $(T - 1)$ $(\frac{T}{2} + E)$ $(\frac{V}{2} + E)$ (B^3) $(\frac{R}{2})$ $(\sqrt{Y})$

Answers

1 MATHS   2 SOLD   3 SOPHIE

Differentiation

- ✺ ⬆ Ask students to devise their own words or sentences.

Subs 3

YEAR 9

Objective covered
Equations, formulae and identities
Substitute numbers into expressions and formulae.

Aim
To practise substituting positive and negative integers into expressions and formulae and begin to extend understanding of index notation to negative and fractional powers.

Resources
Individual whiteboards and pens. To order a pack of 6 dry-wipe whiteboards from Hope Education, Maths supplies for secondary schools phone 08451 202055 and quote SM010/200 (A4) or SP001/200 (A3).

Activity

⊛ Write four letters on the board with their values, for example, $a = -3$, $b = 5$, $c = 8$ and $d = -10$. (Alternatively, ask students to write their own choice of four numbers, then assign a letter to each.)

⊛ Ask students to work in pairs, using whiteboards if you have them, to find the values of the expressions 1 to 10 below.

⊛ Record the names of the first three pairs to get each one correct, and keep a tally of the winners.

1 a^3	2 $\sqrt[3]{c}$	3 b^a	4 $d^3 + c$	5 $\dfrac{a^2}{b}$
6 $\dfrac{d}{a}$	7 $b^3 \div d$	8 $\dfrac{b}{d} - a$	9 $\sqrt{\dfrac{-bc}{d}}$	10 $c^{\frac{1}{a}}$

Answers

1 -27	2 2	3 $5^{-3} = \frac{1}{5^3} = \frac{1}{125}$	4 -992	5 $1\frac{4}{5}$
6 $3\frac{1}{3}$	7 -12.5	8 $2\frac{1}{2}$		9 2 or -2	10 $\frac{1}{2}$

Differentiation

⊛ ⇡ Give students a time limit of, for example, 1 minute per question.

⊛ ⇡ Introduce a points system, say, 10 points each for the first five to get each question right.

71

True or false?

Objective covered

Sequences, functions and graphs
Generate points and plot graphs of linear functions.

Aim

To develop understanding of linear functions of the form $y = mx + c$.

Activity

⊛ Tell students that you want them to write 'T' or 'F' to show whether they think each of the following statements is true or false. When a statement is false, students must correct it. Set a time limit of, say, 1 minute per question.

1 The equation $y = mx + c$ applies to straight line graphs only.

2 In $y = mx + c$, x and y stand for the coordinates of points on the line.

3 m stands for the gradient or steepness of the line.

4 c gives the point where the line cuts the x-axis.

5 When c is zero (so there is no number on its own), the line goes through the origin (0, 0).

6 To get the equation for a line sloping in the opposite direction to $y = mx + c$, c changes sign.

7 If a line goes through the origin and has a gradient of 2, the equation of the line is $y = x + 2$.

8 The line $y = 3$ is a horizontal line.

9 The lines $x = 4$ and $y = 2$ are perpendicular to one another.

10 The smaller the gradient, the steeper the line.

Answers

1 T	2 T
3 T	4 F: c is where the line cuts the y-axis.
5 T	6 F: It is m that changes sign.
7 F: The equation is $y = 2x$.	8 T
9 T	10 F: The smaller the gradient, the less steep the line.

Match up angle facts 1

Objectives covered/aims

Geometrical reasoning: lines, angles and shapes
Use correctly the vocabulary, notation and labelling conventions for lines, angles and shapes.
Identify parallel and perpendicular lines; know the sum of angles at a point and in a triangle, and recognise vertically opposite angles.

Resources

OHP and an OHT prepared as below. Cover the clues/diagrams inside the axes with interlocking cubes or counters.

	1	2	3	4
4	⊲	equilateral triangle	size of a right angle	acute angle
3	△	size of an angle in an equilateral triangle	60°	angles at a point add up to this
2	parallel	90°	360°	↑↑
1	isosceles triangle	vertically opposite angles	▽	⤢

Activity

- Students take turns to call coordinates, e.g. (4, 2) and (1, 2).

- Reveal '↑↑' and 'parallel'. Since these make a pair they are left revealed and the student may pick again having gained 1 point.

- If subsequent chosen pairs of coordinates don't pair up, they are hidden again and it's the next student's turn to pick.

- The winner is the student or team to gain the most points.

Answers

(1, 1) and (3, 1); (1, 2) and (4, 2); (1, 3) and (2, 4); (1, 4) and (4, 4); (2, 1) and (4, 1); (2, 2) and (3, 4); (2, 3) and (3, 3); (3, 2) and (4, 3)

10 questions

Objective covered / aim

Geometrical reasoning: lines, angles and shapes
Use correctly the vocabulary for lines, angles and shapes.

Activity

- ✸ You should have ready a list of ten questions (see below).
- ✸ Divide the class up into 2 or 3 teams. Tell them that jottings are not allowed.
- ✸ One student from each team takes turns in asking for four questions of their choice, for example, numbers 2, 4, 6 and 8.
- ✸ If they get all four questions correct they get 10 points for their team. If they get any wrong, don't say which ones, just tell them they are incorrect. It's then the next team's turn to either choose the same numbers or a different set.
- ✸ Questions you could ask are:

    1 What is the name of an 11-sided shape? (hendecagon)

    2 What is the mathematical name for the shape of a shoe box? (cuboid)

    3 What is the mathematical name for the shape of a Toblerone box? (triangular prism)

    4 What is another name for a tetrahedron? (triangular-based pyramid)

    5 What do you call a triangle with no sides or angles the same? (scalene triangle)

    6 How many lines of symmetry in a parallelogram? (none)

    7 How many degrees are there in a triangle? (180°)

    8 If one of the base angles of an isosceles triangle is 40° what are the other angles? (40° and 100°)

    9 Name four quadrilaterals. (any four)

    10 What is a polygon? (closed 2-D shape with straight sides)

Maths association

Objective covered/aim

Geometrical reasoning: lines, angles and shapes

Use correctly the vocabulary for lines, angles and shapes.

Activity

⊛ Divide the board into two halves, labelled A and B. On each side, at the top, write a different mathematical word, such as 'isosceles' and 'trapezium'.

⊛ Divide the class into two teams, A and B.

⊛ Team members then take turns to come up to the board and write another mathematical word starting with the last letter of the previous word.

⊛ Teams gain 1 point for each word they display on the board – specify a time limit of say 3 minutes. Note the following rules:

- No shouting (or 1 point deducted)

- No running (or 1 point deducted)

- You may pass onto the next student (once only in the game)

- Correct spellings get 2 points (otherwise 1 point, so long as the word can be deciphered and starts and ends with the right letters)

- You may not use any of the other team's words.

Differentiation

⊛ ⇡ Adapt the rules so that incorrect spellings gain no marks.

Hidden maths

Objective covered

Geometrical reasoning: lines, angles and shapes
Use correctly the vocabulary for lines, angles and shapes.

Aim

To practise using the correct vocabulary for lines,
angles and shapes.

Activity

- Divide the class into no more than six groups (otherwise the activity will take too long).

- Each group may choose a topic, but try to end up with about seven topics in total. You could suggest 'shapes', 'lines and angles' and 'anything mathematical' (they'll probably choose football teams etc).

- The chosen topics are then written in a column on the board and one member from each team copies them down.

- You choose a letter and then each team has to think of a word or phrase for each topic starting with the letter chosen. Note the following rules:

  - Time is up when one team has finished writing.

  - Each team gets 1 point for their answer **only** if no other team has the same answer (keep a tally of each team's results on the board).

  - They may not repeat a word, for example, OBTUSE-ANGLED TRIANGLE (for 'shapes') and OBTUSE (for 'lines and angles').

  - They may not choose more than one word for each topic.

2-D versus 3-D

Objective covered

Geometrical reasoning: lines, angles and shapes
Use correctly the vocabulary for shapes.

Aim

To practise using the correct vocabulary for
2-D and 3-D shapes and recognising the
difference between 2-D and 3-D shapes.

Activity

⊛ Sketch randomly on the board the following 2-D and 3-D
shapes (without labels): scalene triangle, trapezium, square,
circle, kite, isosceles triangle, pyramid, hexagonal prism,
cone, octagonal prism.

⊛ Students must first organise them into 2 lists:

3-D	2-D

⊛ By using the first letter of each shape name, ask them to
decipher the hidden word/anagram.

⊛ Give them a clue if they get stuck, 'read the 3-D letters first'.

Answer

3-D	2-D
Cone	**S**calene triangle
Hexagonal prism	**T**rapezium
Octagonal prism	**I**sosceles triangle
Pyramid	**C**ircle
	Kite
	Square

The hidden word is CHOPSTICKS.

Differentiation

⊛ ⬆ Get them to make up their own anagrams using shapes.

Guess the shape

Objective covered

Geometrical reasoning: lines, angles and shapes
Use 2-D representations to visualise 3-D shapes and deduce some of their properties.

Aim

To practise describing accurately the properties of 3-D objects.

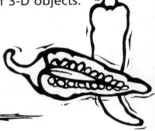

Resources

Ten interlocking cubes per student.

Activity

⊛ Without students seeing, make a 3-D shape out of ten of your own cubes.

⊛ Describe your hidden 3-D model to the class, for them to make. For example, you could make a T-shape and say:

'I started with 2 cubes joined together on the table, one in front of the other. I then added 2 more layers of 2 cubes on top of these to make a cuboid. Finally I joined cubes to the left and right faces of each of the top 2 cubes.'

⊛ See how many hold up the correct arrangement.

Differentiation

⊛ ⬆ Get a student to describe their own 3-D model to the rest of the class.

⊛ ⬆ Get students to work in pairs, describing their arrangements to one another.

Angle acronyms

Objective covered
Geometrical reasoning: lines, angles and shapes
Identify alternate angles and corresponding angles.

Aim
To practise identifying the properties of
angles and parallel and intersecting lines.

Activity
⊛ Divide students into small teams.

⊛ Write these mathematical acronyms on the board for the
class to solve.

1	180 DIAT	2	360 DIAC
3	180 DIASL	4	360 DIAQ
5	90 DIARA	6	5 SIAP
7	AAAE	8	CAAE
9	ZAAAA	10	6 SIAH

⊛ The first team to get all the acronyms right wins.

Answers
1 180 degrees in a triangle
2 360 degrees in a circle
3 180 degrees in a straight line
4 360 degrees in a quadrilateral
5 90 degrees in a right angle
6 5 sides in a pentagon
7 Alternate angles are equal
8 Corresponding angles are
   equal

9 Z angles are alternate angles
10 6 sides in a hexagon

Differentiation
⊛ ⇑ Get students to make one up for the class.

⊛ ⇑ Change 10 to '11 SIAH' (11 sides in a hendecagon).

Match up angle facts 2

Objectives covered / aim

Geometrical reasoning: lines, angles and shapes
Identify alternate angles and corresponding angles.
Know that if two 2-D shapes are congruent,
corresponding sides and angles are equal.

Resources

OHP and an OHT prepared as below. Cover the clues/diagrams inside
the axes with interlocking cubes or counters.

	1	2	3	4
4	parallelogram	isosceles trapezium	right-angled isosceles triangle	✗✗
3	no lines of symmetry	alternate angles	60°	base angles of 45° each
2	quadrilateral with 1 line of symmetry	sum of angles in a quadrilateral	360°	corresponding angles
1	congruent	corresponding sides and angles of 2 shapes are equal	each angle in an equilateral triangle	✗✗

Activity

⚜ Students take turns to call coordinates, e.g. (1, 4) and (1, 3).

⚜ Reveal 'parallelogram' and 'no lines of symmetry'. Since
these make a pair they are left revealed and the student
may pick again having gained 1 point.

⚜ If subsequent chosen pairs of coordinates don't pair up, they
are hidden again and it's the next student's turn to pick.

⚜ The winner is the student or team to gain the most points.

Answers

(1, 1) and (2, 1); (1, 2) and (2, 4); (1, 3) and (1, 4); (2, 2) and (3, 2);
(2, 3) and (4, 1); (3, 1) and (3, 3); (3, 4) and (4, 3); (4, 4) and (4, 2)

Imaginary cubes

Objective covered

Geometrical reasoning: lines, angles and shapes
Know and use geometric properties of cuboids and shapes made from cuboids.

Aim

To practise using the geometric properties of cuboids by visualisation.

Resources

3 by 3 cube made out of 27 interlocking cubes.

Activity

- ❀ Hold up the 3 by 3 cube to the class and get students to imagine a box that will just fit the cube.

- ❀ Now get them to imagine the box is twice as high, three times as long and twice as wide.

- ❀ Ask the class to work out how many small cubes will fit into the new box.

Answer

324 cubes (6 × 6 × 9)

Differentiation

❀ ⬇ Hold up a 2 by 2 cube and ask the same question (4 × 6 × 4 = 96).

Match up angle facts 3

YEAR 9

Objective covered/aim

Geometrical reasoning: lines, angles and shapes
Solve problems using properties of angles, of parallel and intersecting lines, and of triangles and other polygons; understand and apply Pythagoras' theorem.

Resources

OHP and an OHT prepared as below. Cover the clues/diagrams inside the axes with interlocking cubes or counters.

	1	2	3	4
4	exterior angles of a square	exterior angles of a regular pentagon	120°	108°
3	36°	exterior angle of an equilateral triangle	interior angle of an equilateral triangle	90°
2	triangle (sides labelled a, b, c)	interior angle of a regular pentagon	60°	exterior angle of a regular decagon
1	number of sides in a decagon	72°	$b^2 = c^2 - a^2$	10 sides

Activity

- Students take turns to call coordinates, e.g. (2, 3) and (3, 4).

- Reveal 'exterior angle of an equilateral triangle' and '120°'. Since these make a pair they are left revealed and the student may pick again having gained one point.

- If subsequent chosen pairs of coordinates don't pair up, they are hidden again and it's the next student's turn to pick.

- The winner is the student or team to gain the most points.

Answers

(1, 1) and (4, 1); (1, 2) and (3, 1); (1, 3) and (4, 2); (1, 4) and (4, 3); (2, 1) and (2, 4); (2, 2) and (4, 4); (2, 3) and (3, 4); 3, 2) and (3, 3)

Circular register

Objective covered

Geometrical reasoning: lines, angles and shapes
Know the definition of a circle and the names of its parts.

Aim

To practise naming the parts of a circle.

Activity

⊛ Get students to call out a word to do with circles when their name is read out. The next student in the register has to say what the word means. For example:

- student 1 says 'circumference', student 2 says 'perimeter of a circle' or 'the length/distance around the edge'

- student 3 says 'tangent', student 4 says 'a straight line that touches the circumference of the circle'.

⊛ Surprise the class by reading their names starting from the bottom of the register, that is from Z to A.

Differentiation

⊛ ⬇ Use questions on polygons.

⊛ ⬆ Ask the second student to spell the word and then the third student to describe it.

⊛ ⬆ Work it backwards: the first student describes part of a circle, the second person names it and the third person spells it.

Mindful nets

Objective covered
Geometrical reasoning: lines, angles and shapes
Visualise and use 2-D representations of 3-D objects.

Aim
To practise visualising 2-D representations of a cube.

Activity

✹ Draw on the board a labelled net of your choice, such as:

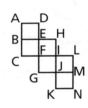

✹ Get the class to imagine folding the net up into a 3-D object and then ask the following questions:

1   What 3-D shape will the net produce?

2   Which point meets with A?

3   Which vertices meet with C?

4   Which edge meets DE?

5   Which face is opposite BEFC?

6   Which face is opposite JMNK?

Answers

1   Cube

2   M

3   G and K

4   EH

5   MLIJ

6   IHEF

Fancy faces

Objective covered
Geometrical reasoning: lines, angles and shapes
Visualise and use 2-D representations of 3-D objects.

Aim
To practise visualising 2-D representations of a cube.

Activity
✲ Draw the following net on the board:

✲ Get students to look carefully at the net (ensuring that they realise it makes a cube) and then see if they can answer the following questions:

   1   Which shape is on the face opposite the circle?

   2   Which shapes are next to the circle?

   3   Which shape is the arrow pointing to?

   4   Which shape is not next to the square?

Answers
1 Scissors
2 All of them except scissors
3 Square
4 Heart

Differentiation
✲ ⬆ Change the shape of the net, to make a hexagonal prism or similar.

Classroom display

Objective covered

Geometrical reasoning: lines, angles and shapes
Visualise and use 2-D representations of 3-D objects.

Aim

To practise drawing 2-D representations of 3-D letters, with appropriate shading for each of the three elevations.

Resources

Isometric (triangular dotty) paper and scissors.

Activity

⊛ Give each student a letter to draw on isometric paper so that when collated, they read '2D REPRESENTATIONS OF 3D OBJECTS' for display.

⊛ Decide on the height of the letters (perhaps 5 cubes high).

⊛ Decide on the shading for the plan, side and front elevations (so that there is some consistency).

⊛ Get students to cut out their letters.

⊛ Result – their work proudly displayed!

Differentiation

⊛ ⬆ Add in the name of the group, for example, 9X1.

Simon says

Objective covered
Transformations
Understand and use the language associated with rotations.

Aim
To use knowledge of angles at a point in context and practise rotating through a number of degrees.

Resources
A4 signs labelled 'North', 'South', 'East' and 'West' in bold, large print.

Activity

- ✸ Pin up signs for north, south, east and west on the four walls of the classroom.

- ✸ Ask all students to stand up and face north.

- ✸ Tell the class that you are going to give them instructions, but they must only follow them if 'Simon says'. Instructions could include 'rotate 90° clockwise', 'turn half a turn', 'turn 45° anticlockwise' etc. Begin some of the instructions with the words 'Simon says'.

- ✸ Anyone who follows an instruction that did not start 'Simon says' is out and must sit down. You could ask one of the students who get caught out to give the next few instructions.

- ✸ The winner is the last student to remain standing.

A, B or C?

Objectives covered/aims

Transformations
Identify all the symmetries of 2-D shapes.
Understand the relationship between regular polygons and their lines of symmetry.

Resources

One individual whiteboard and pen per pair. To order a pack of six dry-wipe whiteboards from Hope Education, Maths supplies for secondary schools, phone 08451 202055 and quote SM010/200 (A4) or SP001/200 (A3).

Activity

⚙ Class members start by standing in pairs.

⚙ Ask multiple choice questions to which pairs reply A, B or C on their whiteboards but they do not display their answer until asked. For example, you could ask:

⚙ 'How many lines of symmetry do the following shapes have?'

1	Parallelogram	A 0	B 1	C 2
2	Isosceles triangle	A 0	B 1	C 2
3	Isosceles trapezium	A 0	B 1	C 2
4	Square	A 1	B 2	C 4
5	Equilateral triangle	A 0	B 2	C 3
6	Regular hexagon	A 0	B 3	C 6
7	Kite	A 0	B 1	C 2
8	Rectangle	A 0	B 1	C 2
9	Regular pentagon	A 0	B 5	C 6
10	Regular dodecagon	A 0	B 10	C 12

⚙ After a time limit, of say 20 seconds, ask all pairs to hold up their whiteboards at the same time.

⚙ Tell those students with the wrong answer to sit down.

⚙ The pair left standing the longest wins.

Answers

1	A	2	B	3	B	4	C	5	C
6	C	7	B	8	C	9	B	10	C

Imaginary axes

Objective covered

Transformations
Transform 2-D shapes by combinations of translations, rotations and reflections.

Aim

To practise transforming shapes.

Resources

A large open space, such as a school hall or playground.
A skipping rope.

Activity

✵ Ask students to spread out in about four rows and eight columns as below.

imaginary
y-axis

skipping rope
x-axis

✵ Students must move places according to your instructions. For example:

- 'Move to your reflection about the *x*-axis.'

- 'Points on the line $y = 1$ swap with points on the line $y = 3$.'

- 'If you are the point (1, 1), rotate 90° anticlockwise about the origin.' (The student must move to (−1, 1).)

✵ Ask a student to specify the next few transformations the class are to make.

Differentiation

✵ ⬆ Discuss the change in coordinates when transformations take place.

Match up squares and roots

Objective covered
Coordinates
Use conventions and notation for 2-D coordinates.

Aim
To practise using 2-D coordinates in the first quadrant and recognising squares and roots.

Resources
OHP and an OHT prepared as below. Cover the numbers inside the axes with interlocking cubes or counters.

4	36	5	9	64
3	9	49	8	81
2	3	6	7	25
1	12	144	16	4
0	1	2	3	4

Activity
- Split the class into teams of 4 or 5 students.

- Teams take turns to call out two pairs of coordinates and then you (or the student) reveal the numbers hidden at these points. For example, a student may pick (1, 2) and (3, 4), to reveal 3 and 9. Since these make a pair ($\sqrt{9} = 3$), the numbers are left revealed and the student may pick again having gained 1 point.

- If subsequent chosen coordinates do not pair up, the numbers are hidden again and it is the next student's turn. If students are observant, it should become easier to find pairs as time goes on.

- The team with the most points at the end wins. You could award bonus points to the team who finish the grid.

Treasure grid

Objective covered/aim

Coordinates
Use conventions and notation for 2-D coordinates in all four quadrants.

Activity

- ⚙ Draw a coordinate grid with all four quadrants on the board.

- ⚙ Secretly give one student the pair of coordinates where the 'treasure' is hidden. This student stands at the front next to the board.

- ⚙ The class take turns at guessing where the treasure is. The student who knows crosses off the class' responses and keeps a tally of how many guesses they have taken.

- ⚙ Whoever finds the treasure, can be the person to place the treasure for the next go.

- ⚙ You could tell the class that they only have ten lives.

Differentiation

- ⚙ ⬇ Use a coordinate grid with only two quadrants.

- ⚙ ⬆ Alternatively, just ask the student at the front of the class to keep a tally of how many questions have been asked, but not to cross off the coordinate pairs. This ensures everyone pays attention.

Colourful axes

Objective covered

Coordinates
Use conventions and notation for 2-D coordinates in all four quadrants.

Aim

To practise plotting 2-D coordinates in the first quadrant.

Resources

Two red and two blue dice.

Activity

- ✸ Tell students to draw *x*- and *y*-axes ranging from 0 to 6.

- ✸ Divide the class into two teams and give each team one red and one blue die.

- ✸ Explain to the class that they are going to use the red die to generate *x*-coordinates and the blue die to generate *y*-coordinates.

- ✸ The team members take turns to roll the two dice and read the coordinates so that everyone in the team can plot them on their axes. For example, if the red die lands on 5 and the blue die lands on 4, all team members must plot the point (5, 4).

- ✸ The first team whose members all have four consecutive points plotted in a line wins.

- ✸ You could adapt this game in various ways to suit your group:

  - Change the number of coordinates that students have to get in a line.

  - Introduce whispering only – you could penalise shouting by making teams start again or wait 10 seconds.

  - You could play the game in more groups and give 10 points to the winning team and 5 points to the team in second place.

Estimating lengths

Objective covered

Measures and mensuration
Use names and abbreviations of units of measurement to measure and estimate in everyday contexts involving length.

Aim

To practise making and justifying estimates for length.

Resources

If available, individual whiteboards and pens are really effective for this activity. To order a pack of six dry-wipe whiteboards from Hope Education, Maths supplies for secondary schools, phone 08451 202055 and quote SM010/200 (A4) or SP001/200 (A3).
A tape measure.

Activity

- Invite a student to pick something in the classroom to measure.

- Ask everyone to estimate the length (it might be worth agreeing on the unit to be used) and write the answer on their whiteboard.

- Invite a student to measure the actual length and see whose estimate was nearest.

- Repeat with other objects and distances, keeping a tally of the winners on the board.

Differentiation

- ⬆ Devise a points system, for example, estimates within 5 cm are worth 10 points and estimates within 10 cm are worth 5 points.

- ⬆ Ask students to work out their percentage of error.

Shapes

Objective covered

Measures and mensuration
Know and use the formula for the area of a rectangle; calculate the perimeter and area of shapes made from rectangles.

Aim

To practise calculating perimeters and areas of shapes.

Activity

⊛ Ask students to produce labelled drawings for each of the following.

1 Draw two different shapes, each with a perimeter of 12 cm.

2 Draw two different shapes, each with an area of 24 cm².

3 Draw a shape with an area of 6 cm² **and** a perimeter of 10 cm.

4 Draw a shape with an area of 24 m² **and** a perimeter of 20 m.

5 Draw a shape with an area of 25 cm² **and** a perimeter of 20 cm.

Answers

1 Simple shapes include a triangle with sides of length 3 cm, 4 cm and 5 cm, a 2 cm by 4 cm rectangle, a 3 cm square and an L-shape with dimensions 3 cm, 1 cm, 1 cm, 2 cm, 2 cm and 3 cm.

2 Any two rectangles whose length and width are factor pairs of 24 will work, for example 4 cm by 6 cm, 2 cm by 12 cm or 8 cm by 3 cm.

3 2 cm by 3 cm rectangle

4 4 m by 6 m rectangle

5 5 cm square

Differentiation

⊛ ⇡ Ask additional questions using algebraic expressions for the perimeter:

6 Draw a shape that has a perimeter of $6x + 12$. ($3x$ by 6 rectangle)

7 Draw a shape that has a perimeter of $6b + 2a$. ($3b$ by a rectangle)

Match up circle facts

Objective covered
Measures and mensuration
Know and use the formulae for the circumference and area of a circle.

Aim

To revise the properties of circles, including the formulae for the circumference and area.

Resources

OHP and an OHT prepared as below. Cover the clues/diagrams inside the axes with interlocking cubes or counters.

	1	2	3	4
4	$2\pi r$	formula for radius of a circle with area, A	formula for diameter of a circle with circumference, C	$\sqrt{\frac{A}{\pi}}$
3	area of a circle	$\frac{C}{\pi}$	part of a circle bounded by an arc and a chord	πd
2	sector	$\frac{C}{2\pi}$	πr^2	tangent
1	formula for radius of a circle with circumference, C	segment	a straight line that touches the circumference	part of a circle enclosed by 2 radii and an arc

Activity

- Students take turns to call coordinates, e.g. (4, 2) and (3, 1).

- Reveal 'tangent' and 'a straight line that touches the circumference'. Since these make a pair they are left revealed and the student may pick again having gained 1 point.

- If subsequent chosen pairs of coordinates don't pair up, they are hidden again and it's the next student's turn to pick.

- The winner is the student or team to gain the most points.

Answers

(1, 1) and (2, 2); (1, 2) and (4, 1); (1, 3) and (3, 2); (1, 4) and (4, 3); (2, 1) and (3, 3); (2, 3) and (3, 4); (2, 4) and (4, 4); (3, 1) and (4, 2)

Which average?

Objective covered

Processing and representing data, using ICT as appropriate
Find summary values that represent the raw data,
and select the statistics most appropriate to the problem.

Aim

To practise planning how to collect data as well as appreciate which statistic is most appropriate to a problem.

Activity

- ✸ Pose the question 'What is the average age of the students in this classroom, in years and months?'

- ✸ Encourage students to discuss how to collect the information effectively.

- ✸ Collect the data as a class and draw up a grouped frequency table together.

- ✸ Add in your age, the older the better!

- ✸ Tell students to estimate the mean and median and find the modal group. They can then discuss which of these best represent the data.

Answer

Your age distorts the mean, making it unrepresentative. The mode and median are often the preferred averages for this type of survey.

Differentiation

- ✸ ⬆ Extend the discussion to whether the interquartile range or range will best represent the spread of data. (The former gets rid of extreme values, so is likely to be more representative.)

- ✸ ⬆ Extend the discussion to talking about the reliability of statistics used in the media.

20 questions

Objective covered
Processing and representing data, using ICT as appropriate
Select, construct and modify lines of best fit by eye.

Aim
To understand what the line of best fit represents.

Activity

- Choose a mathematical phrase, such as 'line of best fit' or 'positive correlation'.

- Secretly give the phrase to one or two class members.

- Tell the rest of the class that they can ask 20 questions to find out what the word or phrase is, to which the students who know the phrase can only answer yes or no.

- It is a good listening exercise for students because they each need to listen to the previous questions so that they do not waste their turn.

- Students will hopefully learn how to ask appropriate questions in order to rule out as many options as possible.

- You could play again, with the class split into two teams. See which team gets the word or phrase first, when taking turns to ask 10 questions each.

Differentiation
- ⬆ Ask a student to choose their own phrase.

Who did better?

Objective covered

Interpreting and discussing results
Compare two simple distributions using the range and one of the mode, median or mean.

Aim

To practise comparing two distributions.

Activity

⊛ Write the following statistics on the board and explain that they were calculated after 5 boys and 5 girls took a maths test, scored out of 20.

> The girls' results had a range of 2 and a mean of 12.

> The boys' results had a range of 19 and a mean of 12.

⊛ Ask students to write down results the boys and girls could have achieved in order to match the statistics given.

⊛ Ask the class to share their answers and discuss which sex did better and how they know.

Answers

The girls' results could have been 11, 12, 12, 12 and 13, for example. The boys' results could have been 1, 11, 12, 16, and 20, for example. The girls' results were more consistent, as indicated by a smaller range. The boys results were more varied, with some achieving top marks and others getting very low marks – this is indicated by the high range. It is difficult to say which sex did better as the means are the same.

Differentiation

⊛ ⬆ Ask students to find other sets of results that would also match the statistics.

Gamble mania

Objective covered
Probability
Use the vocabulary of probability when interpreting the results of an experiment; appreciate that random processes are unpredictable.

Aim
To practise using the ideas and vocabulary associated with probability.

Resources
A pack of ordinary playing cards.

Activity

⚙ Each student begins with an imaginary £50. Explain that you are going to deal the cards, one by one, and that you want them to place bets on what the next card will be.

⚙ Write a few rules on the board, such as minimum bet £5, maximum bet £20, odds for a win are 1:2.

⚙ Ask students to place a bet that the next card is:

- red
- a number less than 10
- a royal card
- lower
- higher.

So, for example, if a student bets £10 and wins on their first go, they get double the money they bet back, as well as their stake, and end up with £70.

⚙ See how many students are still in (not bankrupt) after ten cards are drawn.

Differentiation

⚙ ⬆ Change the odds and/or the minimum and maximum bets.

⚙ ⬇ Keep it simple by just taking bets on whether the next card will be higher/lower.

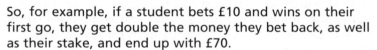

The Grand National

Objective covered/aim

Probability

Estimate probabilities from experimental data; understand that:
- *if an experiment is repeated there may be, and usually will be different outcomes;*
- *increasing the number of times an experiment is repeated generally leads to better estimates of probability.*

Resources

Two ordinary dice.
11 race horses in different colours (you could use paper squares) with the numbers 2–12 written on them.
Blu-Tack.
Fake money (not essential).

Activity

⊛ Stick the 11 horses to the board vertically.

⊛ Draw in a series of fences and the finish line.

⊛ Split the class into teams of five or six.

⊛ Give each team £50 in fake money (or tell them to imagine they have £50).

⊛ Explain to the class, that to start the race you are going to roll two ordinary dice and add the numbers together. This gives the number of a horse, which moves forward by one place. Say that you will continue in this manner, until a horse reaches the finishing line.

⊛ Each team must choose which horse they think will win and bet £50 on it at odds of 1:2.

Differentiation

⊛ ⬆ You could get students to discuss how they could vary the odds for each horse. For example, it could be 1:2 for horses 6, 7 and 8, and 1:5 for all the rest.

Luck of the draw

Objective covered

Probability
Compare experimental and theoretical probabilities in a range of contexts; appreciate the difference between mathematical explanation and experimental evidence.

Aim

To compare experimental and theoretical probabilities.

Resources

Two ordinary dice. Most effective with a giant coloured sponge die. To order, phone 01392 384697 and quote Devon County Council purchasing catalogue number H 71.4950, for a foam cube with dimensions of 155 mm.

Activity

- ⚙ Students need to draw a 3 by 3 grid and fill it with the numbers they think you'll get when you throw 2 dice together and total the scores.

- ⚙ Repeatedly roll 2 ordinary dice and total the scores. Alternatively, throw 2 foam dice to 2 different students for them to catch, place on their desks and shout out the numbers. The class then cross off the total if they have it.

- ⚙ The first student to cross off all their numbers (or 3 in a line for speed) wins.

- ⚙ Students may duplicate numbers and then cross more than one number off at a time. (It may be worth keeping a record of the numbers thrown.)

Differentiation

- ⚙ ⬆ Play the game, discussing theoretical or experimental probabilities.

- ⚙ ⬆ Use differently numbered dice and/or get students to cross off the products of their numbers.

- ⚙ ⬇ Students cross off just one of the number called each roll of the dice.

Published by Letts Educational
4 Grosvenor Place
London
SW1X 7DL
School enquiries: 01539 564910
Parent & student enquiries: 01539 564913
E-mail: mail@lettsed.co.uk
Website: www.letts-educational.com

First published 2002
10 9 8 7 6

ISBN 978 184085 696 5

British Library Cataloguing in Publication Data
A catalogue record for this book is available from the British Library.

Commissioned by Helen Clark
Project management by Vicky Butt
Editing by June Hall and Mark Haslam
Cover design by Ken Vail Graphic Design
Internal design by Ian Foulis & Associates
Illustrations by Ian Foulis & Associates
Cover photo: Jan Cook/Telegraph Colour Library
Production by PDQ
Printed and bound in Great Britain